The Visual Arts in Higher Education

THE VISUAL ARTS

IN HIGHER EDUCATION

A study prepared for the College Art Association of

America under a grant from the Ford Foundation

1966

Library of Congress catalog card number: 66–26247

FOREWORD

The following report on the teaching of art history, on the practice of art, and on the present state of the college or university museum in this country comes, as Mr. Ritchie observes in his preface, just twenty-three years after Robert J. Goldwater's study of 1943 for the College Art Association. During that period our profession, like all other aspects of American education, has undergone phenomenal growth, so that the time has come to reconsider our methods and techniques, as well as our goals.

The Directors of the College Art Association, on behalf of its members, wish to thank Mr. Ritchie and his associates for their prolonged labors in accumulating, compiling, and interpreting the immense amount of data received in response to their questionnaires. The Association has acted only as the disbursal agency for the Ford Foundation grant, and, through its Directors, has transmitted the report to the Foundation. Mr. Ritchie assumed sole responsibility for the scope and conduct of the report. All judgments are his and his colleagues'.

GEORGE HEARD HAMILTON
President of the College Art Association

CONTENTS

PREFACE

At roughly twenty and ten year intervals, three previous studies of some aspects of the teaching of art in American colleges and universities have appeared.[1] Another twenty-year period has now elapsed. The present study, commissioned by the College Art Association of America under a grant from the Ford Foundation, is the result of statistical soundings taken from the academic year 1961–62 and interviews conducted during 1963 and 1964.

As director of the study I chose as my associates Lorenz Eitner, formerly professor of History of Art at the University of Minnesota and now head of the Department of Art and Architecture at Stanford University; Norman L. Rice, dean of the College of Fine Arts, the Carnegie Institute of Technology, Pittsburgh; and, as my assistant, Jules D. Prown, Curator of American Art, the Yale University Art Gallery, and assistant professor of Art History at Yale. From the beginning it was our understanding that the study would confine itself to the history of art, the practice of art (excluding architec-

1. E. Baldwin Smith, *The History of Art in Colleges and Universities of the United States,* Princeton: Princeton University Press, 1912; Priscilla Hiss and Roberta Fansler, *Research in Fine Arts in the Colleges and Universities of the U.S.,* New York: The Carnegie Corporation, 1934; Robert J. Goldwater, "The Teaching of Art in the Colleges of the United States," *College Art Journal,* II, 2, Supplement (May 1943). *The Report of the Committee on the Visual Arts at Harvard University,* published in 1956, contained a study of many other institutions in the United States besides Harvard.

ture), and the art museum, in American colleges and universities.

The study has taken over two years to complete and has proceeded in the following fashion. First, an extensive questionnaire was prepared covering as many facets as possible of the three branches of study. This questionnaire was sent to thirty representative colleges and universities: the University of Arizona, Brown University, Bryn Mawr College, the University of California at Berkeley, the University of California at Los Angeles, the Carnegie Institute of Technology, the University of Chicago, Columbia University, the University of Georgia, Harvard University, the University of Illinois, Indiana University, the State University of Iowa, the University of Kansas, the University of Michigan, the University of Minnesota, the University of Nebraska, New York University, the University of North Carolina, Oberlin College, Ohio State University, the University of Pennsylvania, Princeton University, Smith College, the University of Texas, Vassar College, Washington University-St. Louis, Williams College, the University of Wisconsin, and Yale University.[2]

On receipt of the answers to the questionnaire each of the thirty institutions was visited by one or more members

2. Of these thirty institutions, 12 (40%) are in the Northeast, 12 (40%) in the Midwest, 2 in the South, 2 in the Southwest, 2 on the West Coast (6.7% each). All of the selected institutions in the South, Southwest and West Coast are universities; as are all but one of those in the Midwest and 7 out of 12 of those in the Northeast. 4 out of the 5 selected liberal arts colleges (80%) are in the Northeast; conversely, the 5 selected liberal arts colleges (80%) are in the Northeast; conversely, the largest number of universities studied are located in the Midwest.

All 5 liberal arts colleges are privately supported. Nine of the universities are private and 15 public. None of the 30 institutions has any official religious affiliation.

of our study group. This visitation was designed to check answers to the questionnaire and to administer a series of "opinion" questions which could best be asked in a personal interview with heads of departments and other members of the faculty.

Our next step was to prepare an abbreviated questionnaire which we sent to over seven hundred colleges and universities throughout the United States. Two hundred and thirty-four of the institutions responded. From these responses, together with the first thirty, our statistics and deductions have been compiled.

Some questions we asked proved to have little or no value, usually because they could not be answered with sufficient accuracy, where institutional records were not available or were incomplete; or where, for example, a department was in the process of administrative reorganization and its program was either undecided or in doubt; or, finally, as with so many surveys, where the answers to questions revealed nothing of importance.

In writing up the findings of our study group, for the section on the history of art I have transcribed practically verbatim many of the reports sent to me by Lorenz Eitner, and have added some observations of my own. I am also indebted, in this section, to James Ackerman, Horst Janson, and Sydney Freedberg for communications dealing with visual aid deficiencies and publication limitations. The practice of art section is in the main dependent on Norman Rice's own report to me, with some editorial recasting. The observations on the art museum are entirely my own. I must add, however, that I take full responsibility for this report as a whole, having weighed as judicially as I can my colleagues' conclusions and recommendations. The statistical summaries and tables are the computer's digest of the thousands of pieces of data fed to it under the supervision of Jules Prown, assisted by Mrs. Louise Scott. These two have done a herculean job of tabulating the facts and figures on which most of this report has had to depend.

The analyses, conclusions, criticisms, and recommendations contained in this study have all been made with one end in view: to assist those who profess to teach, practice, or care for art to measure the strengths and weaknesses of the situation in which each of us finds himself today. All our statistics clearly show the enormous expansion which has taken place in college and university art departments and museums in the past twenty years. But if the critical overall view which this report has attempted to record is any indication, those concerned with the arts on the American campus have no reason to feel complacent with whatever progress has been made.

College enrollments are mounting at an alarming rate, but most departments of art history are not attracting or producing a sufficient number of well-trained graduates to meet the present shortage of teachers in the field. The report points to some reasons for this shortage, and makes a number of recommendations concerning it.

By contrast, the study has revealed that the present production of candidates for studio teaching at the college level far exceeds the demand. At the same time we have found a widespread criticism by college teachers of the teaching of art in most secondary schools, without any real acceptance of a share of the responsibility on the part of college teachers for the conditions they deplore. The report has also attempted to measure some of the advantages and disadvantages of college-based studio programs compared with those of the independent art schools. The responses to many of our interviews indicated that the teaching objectives of many undergraduate studio programs are still not sufficiently well defined to permit any definite conclusions as to their precise contribution to a liberal arts curriculum or the quality of the preparation they offer for the education of professional artists.

Finally, in our study of the art museum on the campus, the report notes the fantastic number of new college and university galleries that have been built in this century. Their relative importance for the art historian and the artist is discussed and recommendations dealing with staff, acquisitions, conservation, and building maintenance are made which it is hoped will be of value to museums recently organized or now in the planning stage. The inevitable limitations of university and college museum collections are reported and suggestions are offered for collaborative programs with neighboring public museums.

In broad outline the capsule comments above give some idea of the extent of this study. In dealing with three of the main academic instruments serving the visual arts in America, I am all too conscious that our study group has been forced to limit its investigation to a sampling "in depth," as present-day jargon has it, of a limited number of institutions, that statistics are treacherous indicators of human and artistic problems, and that undoubtedly much of value in the teaching of the arts has escaped our attention. In extenuation, and in all humility, I can only say that, as with all national surveys, the collective limitations of time, energy, and perception of our study group must be taken into account, and all our observations and conclusions must be judged with these shortcomings in mind.

ANDREW C. RITCHIE

The History of Art

INTRODUCTION

The study of American art history is a little over seventy
years old. Long established previously as a separate
"discipline" in Germany and to some degree in France
and Italy, the beginnings of the subject here, in any
systematic sense, date back to Charles Eliot Norton's
lectures at Harvard at the end of the last century. Norton
taught in the English *belles-lettres* tradition of Ruskin
and Pater and left to Harvard an inheritance of critical
connoisseurship, greatly advanced by Bernard Berenson
and Paul J. Sachs, which has distinguished that university's art history studies to this day. Harvard's imprint
has been felt strongly in museums where she has supplied
by far the majority of their directors. Princeton, the other
important fountainhead of American art history scholarship, had from the start an archaeological and early
Christian orientation, befitting the Presbyterian origins
of that college. The late Charles Rufus Morey, Princeton's master teacher, chaired a powerful faculty of art
historians whose imprint has been left on many of the
major art history departments throughout the country.
    Closely following Harvard's and Princeton's depart-
ments came the rise of those at Columbia and New York
University, in the late 1920s and '30s, and Yale's in the
'40s, each with its own particular characteristics. New
York University's Institute of Fine Arts was early given
great distinction by Hitler, who forced so many German

3

art historians to answer the invitation of the late Walter Cook, N.Y.U.'s art history chairman, to take up permanent residence in this country.[1] Columbia's art history development has been less spectacular than N.Y.U.'s, perhaps, but with such eminent teachers as Meyer Schapiro and Millard Meiss, and the recent expansion of the department, it is now responsible for the largest enrollment of graduate art history students in the country. Yale—long famous for its art school, the oldest university art school in the United States—has the youngest art history department among the big universities of the Eastern seaboard. Art history as such did not begin to play a prominent role in the curriculum until the arrival in the late 1930s of two famous visiting French scholars, Marcel Aubert and Henri Focillon.

Outside this eastern complex of art history departments others of considerable distinction have developed at Michigan, Chicago, and Wisconsin, to name only a few. The fact remains, however, that in terms of the production of Ph.D.'s, the five eastern departments mentioned above lead all others in the country. The close association of all five institutions with major museums of art and libraries in New York and New England and their relative closeness to Europe have given them an extraordinary advantage over their associates elsewhere in the country. The following table lists institutions by percentages over one of a total of 453 Ph.D. degrees in art history awarded in the United States from 1930 to 1962:

1. For an excellent account of the refugee art historian in America, see Erwin Panofsky's essay "The History of Art" in *The Cultural Migration, The European Scholar in America,* New York, 1961.

Harvard	28.9
New York University	18.8
Princeton	10.4
Yale	7.5
Columbia	7.3
Chicago	5.1
Iowa	4.9
Ohio	4.0
Michigan	3.8
Wisconsin	2.9
Berkeley	2.4
Byrn Mawr	1.6
Minnesota	1.1

THE SIZE AND GEOGRAPHICAL DISTRIBUTION OF FACULTY

The 264 institutions which responded to our questionnaire include the vast majority, but certainly not quite all, of those teaching art history in the United States. Furthermore, many of the institutions which responded have what are known as "combined" departments of art, where art history is taught both as a separate subject and as a supplement to studio practice. But then again some departments choose to have the studio student taught art history by an artist rather than by an academic art historian. Both kinds of art history teaching are, of course, justified, but for the purposes of this study it has seemed important for us to attempt to estimate the number of full-time and professionally trained academic art historians as distinguished from artists and members of other departments, such as English, history, speech and drama, and philosophy, who may give an occasional course in history or appreciation of art.

From the statistics supplied us, then, and after careful

consideration of the factors above, our most conservative reckoning of the number of full-time art historians teaching in the United States during the academic year 1961–62 comes to some 500, of whom some 300 hold a Ph.D. in the history of art or an equivalent foreign degree.[2]

The geographical distribution of these five hundred art historians, based on a close reading of our statistics, is

2. The figure of 500 was obtained by adding to the totals reported by such institutions as Harvard or Columbia the art history components of the larger "combined departments" (such as Chicago, Indiana, Minnesota) for which we had fairly reliable figures. To this were added the art history faculties of the smaller departments reporting significant enrollments in art history. Since most of the departments in this last category fall into the "combined" type, we had to deduce the sizes of their art history staffs from a variety of indications, such as the number of courses, the enrollments, the number of art majors, the distribution of professorial ranks, and the number of Ph.D.'s (this last not a safe guide, since Ph.D.'s in small departments are frequently art educators, rather than art historians). There is, then, a margin of guesswork in this last portion of the total; but if we have erred, we think we may have erred on the side of caution. Our estimated rough total of 500 (of which the 30 selected schools alone contribute some 300, by way of positively known quantity, while the other 234 schools account for the—somewhat more speculative—remainder of 200) may, in fact, be somewhat too low. According to our calculations, the art history departments of the 30 selected schools (including the art history components of their "combined programs") contained 168 Ph.D.'s, while the remaining 234 schools accounted for the 137 Ph.D.'s. The ratio of Ph.D.'s to total art history faculty in the 30 selected departments (168 to 301) thus turns out to be a little lower than the ratio for the remaining 234 departments (137 to 214). While this seems surprising at first sight, it is not in itself improbable. The large art history departments among the 30 selected schools contain a relatively high proportion of young scholars still working on their degrees (thus Columbia reports the full-time equivalent of 43 art historians, but only 14 Ph.D.'s; Harvard 17 art historians, but only 9 Ph.D.'s). The solitary art historian in a small art department, on the other hand, is likely to be a Ph.D., so that many a small art history staff consists 100 per cent of Ph.D.'s, which is almost never the case in the larger departments.

approximately as follows: about 260 (165 Ph.D.'s) were located in the northeastern states; about 125 (85 Ph.D.'s) in the Midwest; about 65 (30 Ph.D.'s) in the West; and about 50 (25 Ph.D.'s) in the South.

The highest concentration of art history teachers is found in the northeastern states, where nearly all the country's largest departments of art history are located:

	Art history faculty	Ph.D.'s
Columbia	43	14
Yale	20	16
Harvard	17	9
N.Y.U.	17	12
Princeton	17	13
Smith	10	10
Univ. Pennsylvania	10	6

In the Midwest, art history is nearly always part of a combined program, i.e. of a program which includes studio work, and occasionally architecture and art education as well. While the largest art departments in the nation are located in the state universities of midwestern states, their art history faculties are distinctly smaller than those of the eastern universities. The largest midwestern art history faculties are to be found at:

	Art history faculty	Ph.D.'s
Michigan	12	10
Chicago	12	10
Wisconsin	8	3

Of these, only Chicago is a "combined" department. Indiana, Minnesota, Illinois, Iowa, and Oberlin, all of them "combined" departments, closely approach the three largest midwestern departments listed above in size of faculty.

In the western states, art departments are invariably

of the "combined" type if they are not pure studio departments. Only the two large universities have art history faculties which can be compared in size to those of the larger departments in the Northeast and the Midwest:

	Art history faculty	*Ph.D.'s*
University of California, Berkeley	11	6
University of California, Los Angeles	10	6

In the southern states, there are no large departments of art history. The universities of North Carolina (Chapel Hill) and of Georgia, with art history staffs of 4 and 3, respectively, are the largest centers of art history instruction in this region.

If we survey the figures presented above, we obtain a remarkable pattern of distribution. In 1961–62, the eastern third of the United States held 63.1 per cent of the country's teachers of art history, the central third held 24.2 per cent, and the western third 12.7 per cent. Since 1961–62 some changes have occurred, notably in the Western states. But we do not believe that these changes significantly alter the general picture outlined here.

THE SIZE OF THE UNDERGRADUATE ENROLLMENT

It would be useful to know how many undergraduate students in American colleges and universities take courses in the history of art. The evidence contained in the statistics gathered for the present report, unfortunately, does not allow estimating their number with any accuracy. There are several reasons for this. One of them is the unfortunate catchall rubric "combined departments," which offers both art history and studio programs containing, in an inextricable mixture, statistically speaking, the art history and studio course enrollments. The total for this rubric comes to 45,140, a very considerable figure. But how many art history enrollments does it contain? How much of this total is accounted for by studio courses or art education courses? Alas, it is impossible to say.

Despite the difficulties we have encountered in analyzing our statistics, it is important to make an attempt, at least, to grasp the size of the total undergraduate enrollment in art history, for this is one of the main dimensions to which the generalizations and recommendations of the present report have had to be scaled.[3]

Number of students enrolled in art history courses, autumn 1961

(a) The 30 selected departments	14,464
(b) All 264 departments responding	43,342

We think that, despite inaccuracies and exaggerations, this last figure can probably be accepted as being, roughly, true. It is interesting to compare it to the

Number of students enrolled in studio courses, autumn of 1961

(a) The 30 selected departments	12,619
(b) All 264 departments responding	46,358

The comparison at once suggests two facts: the relative weakness of the studio offering in the 30 selected departments, and the preponderance of studio over art history in most of the remaining departments. This preponderance is greater than the difference between the

3. See table 2 of the appendix, *The number of students enrolled in undergraduate courses, autumn 1961.*

figures 43,342 (art history) and 46,358 (studio) would seem to indicate, for the numbers on the lower scholastic levels are weighted in favor of the art history courses which include introductory and survey courses of very large enrollments. Thus the studio enrollment total represents a much *larger number of courses* (the average studio course being much smaller than the average art history course) and hence a much *larger number of teachers* than the art history enrollment total.

Now we come to the mystery of the "combined program." What are we to make of the following figures?

*Number of students enrolled in combined
program, autumn 1961*

(a)	The 30 selected departments	8,398
(b)	All 264 departments reporting	45,140

These totals comprise art history and studio courses (and probably some courses in art education, architecture, home economics, and so on), but in what proportions? Some of the largest individual figures offered under a "combined program," namely, the enrollments of 2,250 and 3,913 reported by the University of California, Berkeley, and the University of California, Los Angeles, respectively, certainly contain a very large—perhaps 50 per cent—proportion of art history enrollments. The same is surely true for Brown (414), Smith (1,069), and Williams (297). But what about Bowling Green (1,054), Brigham Young (1,477), Central Connecticut (1,150), Colorado (1,222), and so forth? We have every reason to suppose that in schools such as these the studio population far outnumbers the art history population, in some cases five to one. It is only necessary to scan the faculties and offerings of these institutions to come to this conclusion. It is our guess, therefore, that no more than one third (15,047), or even one fourth (11,285), of the "combined program" enrollment total can be added to the art history column. We would thus arrive at the following rough approximation:

Number of students enrolled in art history courses, autumn 1961

(a)	Reported by art history program	43,342
(b)	⅓ of total reported by "combined programs"	15,047
	TOTAL	58,389

or

(a)	Reported by art history programs	43,342
(b)	¼ of total reported by "combined programs"	11,285
	TOTAL	54,627

We would estimate the *enrollment* in art history courses in the autumn of 1961, as being anywhere from about 54,500 to 58,500. This does not mean, of course, that this many persons took courses in art history. The figures reported to us refer to enrollments, because these are the only figures that university records show. Since one student can enroll in three or four art history courses in a semester, his head may be counted three or four times. We estimate that the actual number of "bodies" contained in the above figures is probably no greater than 35,000 to, at most, 40,000—but this is in the nature of a *very* rough and highly subjective guess.

Thus, according to our admittedly rough estimate, some 500 teachers of art history confront some 35,000 to 40,000 students in college or university classrooms— a ratio of 1 to 75. Expressed in somewhat different terms, these 500 teachers cover enrollments in art history courses of 54,500 to 58,500, a ratio of about 1 to 110 or 115. In looking at these ratios, we must bear in mind that the 264 schools reported an average total enrollment in survey courses of 25,988. This means that almost half the student population of art history courses occurs in the large introductory or survey courses.

UNDERGRADUATE MAJORS

The total enrollments in art history courses are impressive, even if allowance is made for the share of this total of survey courses or of courses that must be considered to be on the fringes of art history.

All the more surprising is the very small number of undergraduates specializing in the history of art.[4] The art history programs of the 30 selected schools reported a total of 299 art history majors in 1961–62—a figure remarkably small when it is recalled that this includes the art history majors in such departments as Chicago, Columbia, Harvard, Michigan, New York University, Princeton, and Yale. The art history programs of the remaining 234 schools reported 332 majors. The "combined programs" of the 30 selected schools reported 424 majors: one of the totals in our statistical tabulation that demand, but also defy, precise analysis. There is practically no such thing as a "combined" art major. Students in the "combined" departments usually major either in art history or studio practice. The total of 424 majors— covering such departments as Brown, Berkeley, U.C.L.A., Iowa, Minnesota, Nebraska, and Smith— must be broken down into an art history and a studio component, but we know of no accurate way of doing this. By way of rough and highly subjective guess, we estimate that the figure of 424 includes about 150–200 art history majors, almost certainly not more than that.

4. See table 3, *Number of students graduating with a major in art history, studio program, or combined program.*

As for the "combined" majors, 1,439 of them, reported by the remaining 234 departments (most of which are studio-oriented), we estimate that they include no more than 250 to 275 true art history majors. The national total of art history majors in 1961–62 would therefore come to roughly 1,025 to 1,100. Thus, of about 54,500 to 58,500 enrollments in art history courses, only a relative few represent art history majors. If we are correct in estimating that the enrollments in art history courses represent some 35,000 to 40,000 individual students, then students *taking courses* in art history outnumber students *majoring* in art history something between 32 and 39 to 1. Or, expressed somewhat differently, the art historian addressing a class of 100 upperclassmen may, in fact, be speaking to no more than an average of 3 students actually majoring in the history of art. And if approximately one half of the majors are graduating seniors, then we produced about 550 art history majors in 1962.

If we look a little more closely at the numbers of graduating majors in art history reported by individual departments, fresh surprises come to light: Harvard (66) and Columbia (42), not surprisingly, head the list; but they are immediately followed by Skidmore (37), Wellesley (34), Kent State (30), and Arizona (22). New York University (Washington Square) reports only 20 majors, Wheaton 16, Michigan 15, and William and Mary 15. Yale follows with 13 majors and Princeton 10. Pennsylvania reports only 8 art history majors, Bryn Mawr only 6, but these are still impressive totals compared to Chicago's 2. The huge departments of the Midwest report some of the smallest figures: Illinois (the largest art department with the largest budget in the nation) reports 2 art history majors, Ohio 4, Kansas 4,

Wisconsin 5, and Indiana 6. It is interesting to compare the numbers of art history majors, in the academic year 1961–62, with the numbers of studio majors.

	Art history majors	Studio majors
Illinois	2	78
Ohio	4	69
Kansas	4	39
Texas	8	55
Wisconsin	5	50
Indiana	6	30
TOTAL	29	321

The ratio for these departments is something like 11 studio majors to 1 art history major. We think this gives us clues to the interpretation of totals of majors reported by such "combined" programs as Berkeley (70), U.C.L.A. (146), and Iowa (28)—the art history components in them must be very small.

From the statistical analysis above the facts allow only one conclusion: though art history courses are popular with general students, they lure very few of them into specialized study. What can the reason be? It is noteworthy, at any rate, that the condition exists in excellent departments, as well as in indifferent ones. It is also noteworthy that, in a decade in which all enrollments show a spectacular increase, some departments report a decline in the number of art history majors:

	1961	1951	1941
Bryn Mawr	6	7	9
Harvard	66	73	
Oberlin	7	8	15
Ohio	4	6	
Vassar	9	18	21

GRADUATE STUDY IN THE
HISTORY OF ART

For a listing of total enrollment figures for 1961–62 the reader is referred to table 5. It must be said at once that this table does not provide us with an accurate picture of graduate study programs for all the universities studied, since some institutions reported only total *course* enrollment and others actually counted heads of students enrolled regardless of the number of courses they took. The number of Ph.D. candidates thus furnishes a more reliable index to the actual sizes of graduate programs. Listed according to numbers of candidates in 1961–62, the programs were as follows:

Harvard	70
New York University	60
Columbia	33
Yale	20
Univ. Pennsylvania	11
Iowa	11
Univ. of Michigan	9
Univ. of California, Berkeley	8
Minnesota	8
Univ. of California, Los Angeles	5
Wisconsin	5
Chicago	5
Princeton	3

TOTAL   248

Another way of rating the graduate programs in art history is by their productivity, in other words, their *output* of Ph.D.'s.

Number of doctorates in art history awarded between
1930 and 1962

	Total	1930–39	1940–49	1950–59	1960–62
Harvard	133	25	29	65	14
N.Y.U.	57	5	9	29	14
Princeton	47	6	6	25	10
Yale	34	—	9	17	8
Columbia	33	1	3	15	15
Michigan	17	—	4	9	4
Wisconsin	14	3	2	6	3
Berkeley	11	—	—	6	5
Chicago	23	4	4	14	1

The nine schools listed thus produced 354 Ph.D.'s in the history of art in the past third of a century. The output of all the other schools offering Ph.D.'s—of the 264 departments reached by our survey, apparently only 20 have ever granted a Ph.D. degree—adds slightly less than 100 to this total. Thus, Minnesota until 1962 produced only 5 Ph.D.'s, Washington University only 1, Pennsylvania only 1, and so forth.

In estimating the total strength of the teaching force in art history we put the figure of teachers at about 500 and the number of Ph.D.'s included in this total at about 300. This agrees rather closely with the entire output of American departments for 1930–63. Not all the Ph.D.'s teaching art history in America are of that vintage, of course, nor do all of them hold American doctorates. On the other hand, a number of those who earned their Ph.D. in 1930–63 have chosen professions other than teaching (museum work, for example), or have left teaching for some reason. The foreign doctorates and the doctorates acquired before 1930 thus appear to balance fairly precisely the number of Ph.D.'s who did not enter (or were lost to) the teaching profession.

It has taken more than 30 years to produce 453 Ph.D.'s in the history of art. The pending Ph.D. candidacies for 1962, listed on page 15, and representing the 13 departments reporting the largest graduate enrollments, numbered 248. If these Ph.D. candidates were all to receive their degrees and were all to go into teaching—which is very unlikely, of course—they would increase the number of Ph.D.'s in American art departments by about 55 per cent.

Actually, the annual "production" of Ph.D.'s is very much smaller than the large number of current candidacies would indicate, for many of these will remain pending for a long time to come, if not forever. But the general increase in the number of doctorates is remarkable, although, of course, it must be measured against the enormous increase, present and potential in general college enrollments. During the 1930s, the number of doctorates in art history awarded by American universities and colleges in an average year was around 4, in the '40s it had increased to about 6, in the '50s it rose steeply to around 17, and during the '60s it seems to be close to 26. The increase since the '30s has thus been roughly sixfold: the current decade ought to produce at least 300 Ph.D.'s in the history of art.

THE COURSE OFFERING

The following remarks are purely concerned with the *quantity,* not the *quality* of the offering. According to the figures furnished to us by the 264 departments, the following were the *largest* course offerings:

Undergraduate course offerings, ranked by size of offering

	Ancient	Medieval	Renaissance	17th–18th century	19th century	20th century	Far Eastern	Near Eastern	American	Methods
Univ. Michigan	7	6	6	3	4	4	7ʼ	2	5	4
U.C.L.A.	2	3	7	5	2	2	3	1	1	2
Harvard	5	3	5	3	2	1	3	1	2	–
Ohio	3	2	4	3	1	2	4	–	2	3
Berkeley	4	3	4	1	1	–	4	2	1	1

Graduate course offerings, ranked by size of offering

	Ancient	Medieval	Renaissance	17th–18th century	19th century	20th century	Far Eastern	Near Eastern	American	Methods
Columbia	27	14	14	16	6	7	9	9	4	3
Chicago	10	10	10	13	11	3	9	–	–	–
N.Y.U.	6	10	17	10	5	5	4	1	2	–
Univ. Penn.	5	5	7	7	4	2	7	–	8	1
Indiana	7	8	3	1	2	4	3	–	–	–
Univ. Michigan	3	6	2	5	2	1	8	4	–	2
Harvard	2	1	4	2	3	–	2	–	–	1
Princeton	4	2	6	2	1	–	3	–	1	1
Yale	4	2	2	2	1	2	1	–	1	1

The salient fact to be observed by comparing the under-graduate and graduate figures is the much larger quantity and variety of the offerings at the graduate level. Courses are small, presumably brief, and rotate with greater fre-quency than the basic undergraduate courses which are constantly repeated from season to season.

In surveying the total offering in the history of art, for the two years preceding 1962 as listed in the course cata-logues of the 264 departments responding, we obtain the following picture:

Distribution of undergraduate courses in the history of art, ranked by size of offering in each area

	Number of courses
Renaissance	294
Ancient	217
19th century	187
Medieval	180
20th century	165
17th–18th century	149
American	144
Far Eastern	119
Methodology	45
Latin American	33
Prints	29
Primitive and exotic	20
Near Eastern	19
Museology	4
"Other"	370
TOTAL	1,975

A somewhat different ranking obtains for graduate courses:

Distribution of graduate courses in the history of art, ranked by size of offering in each area

	Number of courses
Renaissance	111
Ancient	86
Medieval	84
17th–18th century	81
19th century	53
Methodology	49
20th century	47
American	30
Primitive and exotic	20
Museology	17
Far Eastern	22
Near Eastern	16
Prints	11
Latin American	9
"Other"	66
TOTAL	702

It is interesting to compare these tabulations with a similar one, restricted to fifty schools, compiled by Robert J. Goldwater in 1940 (in which no distinction was made between undergraduate and graduate courses.)[5]

5. Robert J. Goldwater, "The Teaching of Art in the Colleges of the United States," *College Art Journal,* II, 2, Supplement (May 1943).

Distribution of courses in the history of art (1940)

	Number of courses
Classical	128
Medieval	107
Renaissance	104
Baroque	56
Modern	55
American	40
TOTAL	490

Courses in Classical art, Goldwater noted, had been the most numerous since 1900, a fact which reflects the early development of the art history curriculum as an offshoot of classics and philology. By 1940, courses in Medieval art, steadily on the increase since 1925, had edged up to second place, having overtaken the much more slowly increasing offering in Renaissance art. This growing strength in Medieval art, in turn, expressed the particular American emphasis on medieval studies during the generation of Kingsley Porter and Rufus Morey. The sudden growth to predominance of Renaissance studies, after 1940, almost certainly was due to the arrival of the refugee scholars in the late 1930s, which not only gave a great impetus to the teaching of art history in this country, but also imparted to it a perceptible bent toward the study of Renaissance and Baroque art. The most marked change since 1940, in addition to the rise of Renaissance studies to first place, is the increase in courses in modern, i.e. nineteenth- and twentieth-century art. Interestingly enough, this is less apparent in the grad-

uate curriculum of 1961–62 than in the undergraduate.
It can be said, in fact, that the graduate curriculum is
more "conservative" in its evolution, resembling somewhat more closely the pattern of 1940 in its relative
emphasis on the different periods than does the undergraduate curriculum.

The Goldwater study was based on a sampling of 50
schools, while the present study is based on information
furnished by 264 schools. It is difficult, therefore, to compare the totals in the Goldwater study with the totals of
our study in such a way as to express their true significance. Both sets of totals are incomplete, in that they
omit a number of departments offering art history, but it
is impossible to determine to what degree they are incomplete. The 50 schools reporting to Goldwater on their
offerings in 1940 certainly represented the preponderant
majority of schools which offered substantial programs
in art history during that year. Many of the schools
responding to our study of 1962 did not offer any art
history in 1940 and would not have affected the totals
of the Goldwater study, even if they had been included.
Bearing these uncertainties in mind, we may weigh the
evidence of the totals:

Total number of courses in the history of art
(graduate and undergraduate)

1940
Goldwater study (selection of 50 departments)   795

1961–62
CAA study (264 departments reporting)   2,637

Allowing for the fact that the Goldwater total rests on
a more limited base of inquiry and is more incomplete

than ours, we may venture the rough guess that the figures for 1961 indicate a *doubling* of the offering in art history in the course of the twenty-year interval since 1940. Actually, this corresponds to the rate of growth for the period between 1920 and 1940 as reported by the 50 departments of the Goldwater study: the increase in the number of courses was from 380 in 1920 to 795 in 1940. In trying to form an approximate idea of the growth of art history instruction over the past decades and in estimating the probable future rate of growth, we shall not go far wrong, we believe, if we assume that the academic course offering in the history of art *approximately doubles every twenty years*. This, at least, is suggested by what figures we have for the period from 1900 until the present. One further comment. The Goldwater table of course distribution makes no mention of Oriental and non-Western art studies, presumably because they were relatively unimportant in 1940. In 1961–62 this is no longer so, as our table shows. The Second World War's having been fought in all corners of the globe no doubt had its effect on the increased attention now being given in many of our universities to non-Western area studies, particularly African and Asian. Even before the war important collections of African, Oceanic, and Asian art were being assembled in American public and private collections and with the contraction of the market in European art the impetus to collect non-Western art has been enforced. The Boston Museum of Fine Arts, following the old New England China trade and the transcendental musings of some of her theologians and philosophers, early took the lead in collecting Far Eastern art and the Harvard art history curriculum has long been strong in this department.

Other museums in the East with important Far Eastern collections include those in New York, Brooklyn, Yale University, Philadelphia, Baltimore, and Washington, D.C. There are also important Far Eastern collections in Cleveland, Chicago, Kansas City, Minneapolis, and San Francisco. And within recent years the Museum of Primitive Art was founded in New York. Language difficulties still present a serious brake on non-Western art studies. There is now, however, a considerable effort being made, particularly in departments of Asian studies, to pierce the language barrier and the opening up of these vast new fields for art historical research is undoubtedly imminent and long overdue. A contributing factor in this aroused interest in African and Asian art has undoubtedly been the post-Impressionist painters' preoccupation with "primitive" art and the more recent interest of some abstract artists in Zen Buddhist principles of behavior and creation.

Finally, whatever the exact figures, any statistical comparison between the course offerings of 1940 and that of 1961 will suggest at first sight that great progress has been achieved. It is evident that more teachers serve more students and that the course offering has grown. If quantity provides some measure of quality, art history at American universities and colleges would appear to be in a flourishing state. But quantities do not provide a reliable measure, and the true picture of the present condition of art history in America can be drawn only if statistical "facts" are supplemented by judgments of value. These, inevitably, must be subjective to a large degree, and are more difficult to support by proof or demonstration.

SURVEY COURSES

The first section of our printed questionnaire for art history sent to the thirty selected institutions dealt with the undergraduate program of teaching. Our first questions had to do with the introductory survey course or courses, the type of course given (historical survey or non-historical, topical survey), average enrollment, and ranks of faculty members participating.[6]

Number of departments giving historical survey courses: 28 (1 year course, 18; semester or quarter, 12)

Number of departments giving non-historical survey courses: 2 (1 year, 1; semester, 1)

Number of departments giving both historical and non-historical courses: 10 (1 year, 4; semester or quarter, 6)

Average class enrollment	Art history
1961–62	193.7
1950–51	159.8
1940–41	110.1

Rank participating in each course (1961–62)

professors	1.9	instructors	2.1
associate professors	1.5	assistant instructors	4.6
assistant professors	2.1	lecturers	1.2

6. The response to our questions on the survey course by the remaining 234 of the 264 institutions was somewhat ambiguous. Many departments seem to have been in doubt as to just what was meant by our asking them to distinguish between a "non-historical" and an "historical survey."

From our statistics one can draw three pretty firm conclusions: (1) the average size of classes has been on the steady increase from 1940 to 1962; (2) the chronological, historical survey course is favored over the non-historical, topical course by 28 to 2, although ten of the thirty departments favor a mixture of both kinds of surveys; (3) the heavier "teaching load" (an unhappy term) is borne by assistant professors and instructors.

Our assumption is that the information we gathered from our respondents referred mainly to art history surveys, chronological in their coverage, and varying widely in the density and detail of their coverage. The total of 25,988, recorded from our questionnaire, for "the average current—1961–62—enrollment in the introductory historical survey courses" is certainly incomplete if not meaningless, since we do not know whether this figure includes totals for *repeated* courses or only averages for the individual, typical course.

A common introductory offering is the coupling of a principles course with a brief historical survey: the principles course (lasting only a quarter or semester) introduces students to basic concepts of form, style, meaning, and the like; armed with these, they go on to consider the historical development of art. Thus:

First quarter:	Introduction to the Principles of Art ("non-historical")
Second quarter:	Survey of Art History—Ancient and Medieval Art
Third quarter:	Survey of Art History—Renaissance and Modern Art

The value of the "non-historical" introductory course, for students intending to go on with art, as well as for the general student, is that it deals, or ought to deal, with fundamental questions—with questions of style, of representation, of meaning, of diverse influences on art, and so on—which are apt not to come up again in the more "advanced" courses, though a knowledge of them will be taken for granted. It is undoubtedly true that in the academic teaching of art history, the minutiae are treated better, and at much greater length, than the fundamentals, which tend to be either dismissed altogether, or dealt with very summarily on the lowest level. Questions of quality (which are awkward to deal with, but which deeply interest students), problems in connoisseurship (which are difficult to discuss before large classes and with the aid of mere slides), and a host of other important and fundamental issues are hard to cover adequately in art history courses, partly because of technical difficulties, partly because an extended and systematic discussion of them is not easy to fit into the congested timetable of an historical course. The "principles course", superficial and brief though it tends to be, is nevertheless of value because it gives relatively greater scope for such an extended and systematic discussion of general topics than do purely historical surveys.

Goldwater mentions, in his study of 1940, that the giving of survey courses was a matter of controversy. This, we think, is no longer true. Both the topical and the chronological/historical survey course, and frequently a combination of the two, are firmly entrenched in nearly all departments. In some they constitute the main business and are, as far as the college at large is concerned, the department's *raison d'être*. Wherever they are given, they present the problems that normally attend large courses: problems of staffing (particularly with teaching assistants and readers), of space and equipment, of testing (how, without overloading the staff, can 500–600 examination papers be read and graded within a reasonable time), and of general academic management. Good, brief histories of art are now available but there exist few satisfactory texts for the principles courses, a handicap some teachers have tried to overcome by producing their own texts, syllabi, or manuals.

TEACHING

In surveying the problems and estimating the needs which confront academic art history in the United States, it is useful to keep separate the areas of general teaching and of professional scholarship, because they differ in important ways.

The teaching of art history has become a large enterprise during the past twenty years. It now involves several thousand instructors in some seven hundred schools. But, certainly, only relatively few of these can be considered as specialists in the history of art. Of the tens of thousands of students who take courses in the history of art during any given year, the vast majority are only transients, the population of survey courses and humanities programs.

While it is true that art history has established itself as a regular part of the undergraduate curriculum, its role is still rather a modest one. It serves far more often as a supplement to other programs than as a field of specialization. On this score, the statistics of our study leave little doubt. The number of undergraduates who elect art history as their major (even at universities which offer excellent courses) has remained surprisingly small throughout the years and appears not to be growing.

In the meantime, survey courses will continue to be the bread and butter of most art departments. There is little glory to be gained by them. To the scholar they are often a drudgery and distraction. But their cultural importance must not be underrated. There must be hundreds of thousands of Americans who have gained what knowledge they have of art through these courses. If the American audience for art has enormously increased in recent years, this is partly because of the mass courses in art offered by the universities and colleges. The new audience for art is almost wholly college-bred, and in its education the survey course has had a dominant share.

The main problem here is one of quality. There is a great need for better instruction, in other words, for better-trained teachers and better instruments of teaching. Understandably enough, the largest courses most often fall to the lot of the youngest or of the least distinguished members of the faculty. As a result, many of them are poorly taught. The running of large survey courses is certainly not the proper employment of productive scholars; but it is too important to be left to the inexperienced or ineffectual. Since the conditions which make for large enrollments in these courses are not likely to change soon, it is probable that large numbers of teachers will continue to be busy with them.

Many of the present difficulties with introductory and survey courses result from the simple fact that they are a chore with which departments do not burden their more distinguished members. The more illustrious the faculty, the farther removed from such teaching chores are its senior professors apt to be. This may account for the fact that even in universities which boast excellent art departments, very few undergraduates elect to major in art history. The reason is often an introductory course which acts as a barrier, rather than an invitation to further study in art. Many art historians have an understandable dislike of survey courses, and are not at all disinclined to keep the undergraduate art history program small. They argue that the really able undergraduate determined to pursue studies in the history of art will not be deterred by a wretched introductory course or by boring initial surveys. On the contrary, his determination and seriousness will be tested by them; if he has the stamina to suffer through them, he will be more likely to persevere until the end.

There may be something to be said for this view, as far as the small, dedicated core of strongly art-history-minded undergraduates is concerned. But for students in general, whose only exposure to art history the survey courses are likely to be, it opens a dismal perspective. The survey and introductory courses, however unpalatable to the scholar, have (or should have) a wide cultural impact on our college-bred society. If the best art historians dedicate themselves too exclusively to highly specialized teaching, the lower-level courses will not reflect the best our discipline has to offer. And since art history is not for art historians only, this would be a pity.

The present shape of academic art history is rather like that of an hourglass: a wide bottom (the basic courses with their mass population), a fairly wide top (the graduate courses with their relatively large enrollments, at least in those universities which emphasize graduate work), and between them a narrow waist—the remarkably small number of undergraduate majors. What is the explanation for the unpopularity of art history as an undergraduate major? The reason given by some department chairmen is that students are influenced in their election of a major by parental advice or attitudes, and that many parents still look with alarm on the choice of an impractical or unprofitable field of specialization. There may be something to this argument but, in our opinion, not much. For one thing, the election of an undergraduate major is not looked upon by most students as committing them to any particular professional future. For another, the arts and humanities have acquired considerable prestige of their own. Parents, at least those in the middle- or upper-income groups, insofar as they exert any influence, seem quite tolerant of them and, if their children be girls, often actually favor cultural over practical areas of study. There has been in recent years a decline in the enrollments of schools of business and engineering, and a corresponding increase in the enrollments of humanities colleges. So far as we can see, art history *as an undergraduate major,* does not appear to have profited from this trend. As we have indicated above, some departments (including Harvard, Vassar, Oberlin, Bryn Mawr) actually report a drop in the number of senior majors. Why, if history attracts so many, does art history appeal to so few?

A second and, if our inquiries are reliable, more important reason is that men in particular, and some women, too, have the idea that to specialize in the arts one must possess talents and sensitivities of a very unusual sort. Art calls up in their minds the image, or caricature, of the "aesthete." The affectations and snobbisms which surround some parts of the art establishment have helped to keep alive this ancient prejudice.

The Comparative Costs of Studio and Art History Instruction

The art department budgets for 1961–62 of twenty-nine selected institutions responding ranged from $526,000 (a combined studio and art history department in the Midwest) down to $185,000 (a major university art history department in the East). Ten of the combined departments, all state-supported institutions, are in the Midwest or West and three of these have the highest recorded budgets. In most combined departments there is every indication that the cost of studio instruction far exceeds that of art history. It is also notable that many of the "pure" studio department budgets far exceed most of the "pure" art history department budgets. Where separate studio and art history department budgets can be compared, as in two midwestern institutions, both having an unusually strong art history reputation, studio costs are over twice those of art history, in one instance, and, in the second, three times as much.

Combined departments are a midwestern and western phenomenon. The type is rare in the East, where art history, usually "pure," predominates. Pure studio departments are also found for the most part in the Midwest or West. Where pure studio departments occur in the East, they tend to be smaller and less costly than the art history departments of their universities.

The main reason for the wide difference in cost between art history and studio instruction is the need for a larger staff for the latter. Studio classes must be relatively small, the student-teacher ratio is therefore more favorable than in art history instruction. An additional reason for the proliferation of studio faculties is the ever-increasing number of technical specialties which large departments seek to cover—jewelry making, printmaking, drawing, sculpture, painting—each of which requires a specialist or a group of specialists. Thus, when art history and studio are developed side by side in the same department, and no effort is made to impose a check on the growth of either, the studio faculty inevitably outgrows the art history faculty. A serious consequence of this imbalance is that it can lead to the political and academic control of the department by the studio component and, in time, to the budgetary and political (and often academic) shrinkage of the art history component.[7]

THE COST OF ART HISTORY INSTRUCTION: SALARIES IN RELATION TO SUPPLIES AND EQUIPMENT

The cost of art history instruction can be read most clearly in the budget figures furnished by the "pure" art history departments (it is nearly impossible to disentangle the art history components from the total budgets of combined departments). It is very apparent that budget size is closely related to staff size: salaries and wages account for very nearly the whole of the budgets, supplies and equipment for remarkably little. Figures for the latter are given in the following tabulation:

7. The midwestern and western emphasis on studio instruction on the campus can no doubt also be explained by the early emphasis in land grant colleges on the vocational value of education. The *making* of paintings and sculpture and other works of art seems inevitably to have had a greater appeal to Congressmen and administrators than the giving of courses in art history, with their purely theoretical and verbal implications. The slow growth of art history departments in some state universities is one result of this situation.

1961–62	Art book holdings	Art book budget[8]	Slide holdings (black & white)	Slide holdings (color)	Slide budget	Photograph holdings	Photograph budget
Arizona	22,000	$ 500	7,000	8,000	$ 300	1,000	$ 0
Brown	26,000	4,100	20,000	14,000	1,000	30,000	400
Bryn Mawr	15,000	6,000	32,000	6,000	500	24,000	100
Berkeley	90,000	40,000	107,000	23,000	1,200	19,000	1,000
U.C.L.A.	32,000	5,500	44,000	32,000	3,000	11,000	300
Carnegie Institute	20,000	8,000	16,000	10,000	1,500	1,000	0
Chicago	34,000	9,700	79,000	800	4,000	300,000	3,500
Columbia	99,000	30,000	122,000	10,000	2,000	26,000	2,500
Georgia	10,000	4,800	30,000	20,000	500	2,000	0
Harvard	200,000	20,000	82,000	15,000	7,000	750,000	8,500
Illinois	45,000	6,000	34,000	7,000	?	29,000	?
Indiana	13,000	700	32,000	8,000	3,600	1,000	1,200
Iowa	23,000	1,800	50,000	12,000	2,500	40,000	500
Kansas	15,000	3,800	25,000	25,000	2,000	27,000	500
Michigan	44,000	9,500	59,000	22,000	2,700	48,000	1,600
Minnesota	50,000	10,000	45,000	16,000	2,300	80,000	900
Nebraska	9,000	1,700	17,000	1,000	200	4,000	0

N.Y.U.	57,000	24,000	157,000	6,000	9,700	4,000	100
North Carolina	16,000	5,000	18,000	5,000	1,800	8,000	2,000
Oberlin	22,000	5,000	99,000	11,000	400	20,000	0
Ohio State	16,000	5,900	35,000	20,000	3,000	35,000	200
Pennsylvania	12,000	3,500	49,000	29,000	700	11,000	1,000
Princeton	65,000	39,500	90,000	17,000	4,000	650,000	1,200
Smith	18,000	3,600	60,000	15,000	500	40,000	900
Texas	14,000	14,400	60,000	30,000	3,000	10,000	?
Vassar	18,000	3,000	38,000	5,000	1,800	28,000	1,000
Washington (St. Louis)	25,000	12,000	5,000	4,000	800	4,000	0
Williams	10,000	1,900	20,000	21,000	1,800	1,000	200
Wisconsin	27,000	6,400	60,000	40,000	3,500	6,000	200
Yale	60,000	7,000	100,000	22,000	4,400	108,000	1,600
High	200,000	40,000	157,000	40,000	9,700	650,000	8,500
Low	9,000	500	5,000	800	200	1,000	0

35

8. It should be noted that the appropriations listed here do not indicate whether the budget applies to the whole university library, the art library only, to new book titles only, or to all titles, including serial publications. The totals given must be evaluated with these undefined budgetary differences in mind.

An analysis of the table above reveals that of the thirty institutions responding the highest proportion of any one budget allotted to the acquisition of lantern slides was 3.6 per cent and to art books 12.4 per cent.[9] The budget for photographs, it will be noted, is insignificant in all but a few departments. The above statistics also prove that the departments specializing in the history of art and carrying full graduate programs in the main benefit from large book budgets. Large "combined" departments, on the other hand, spend relatively little on books. There are, however, notable exceptions to both these rules. In any case, it can be said that expenditures for books and slides combined, even in the best-equipped departments under study, in 1961–62 very rarely exceeded 15 per cent of the total of any one budget.

Summing up the evidence available to us, it appears that the high cost of art books, slides, and photographs does not burden the budgets of most art history programs as much as it should. The only exceptions are young and fast-growing departments attempting to overcome serious inadequacies in libraries or slide collections by means of a "crash-program" of purchasing. But these are far outnumbered by the very numerous departments, the budgets of which show astonishingly small expenditures for photographs, slides, and books. Since books and slides *are* in fact expensive items, and since book prices, at any rate, are inelastic (while the cost of slides shows wide variations), we are fairly certain that this situation can only mean that many art history departments are not

9. This percentage must be read with the following qualifications in mind: in most colleges and universities the art department receives a yearly allotment of the general library budget and this item is not carried in the department's own budget. Some departments also have access to special or outside funds for books.

doing an adequate job in building their libraries and slide collections. The reasons for this inadequacy are not always clear. Many departments undoubtedly have been unable to secure sufficient funds for the job of building they would like to do. Other departments may be indifferent or resigned to a low budget for teaching and research tools. It is noticeable that some of the richest departments have the smallest budgets for books and slides. Building a library or a good slide collection requires planning, knowledge, and work, and a very strong incentive. A department's vigor can be measured to a large extent by the rate of growth of its library and of its slide collection. If a fair-sized department spends less than $2,000 on slides per annum, this may signify either that it has access to a source of unusually cheap slides, or that the courses being taught in it stay much the same year after year. If such a department spends less than $5,000 yearly on books, it is probably not keeping up with current publications, and its library is likely to become less and less complete as the years pass.[10]

Departmental budgets may reflect not so much the needs of departments as their interests and ambitions. Except for very small departments in poverty-stricken schools, most art departments ought to be able to command the sums which are necessary for the acquisition and maintenance of an adequate slide collection. All departments offering graduate work are under a moral obligation to their students, it seems to us, to secure the sums which are necessary for the building and maintenance of an adequate library.

10. In this connection see the standards established for small departments by the Southeast College Art Conference, published in the spring 1965 *Art Journal*.

Problems and Needs of the Profession

There are many serious problems confronting the art history profession in America. Two stand out above all the others, many of which are related to these two as their contributing causes or their results:

(1) the country-wide shortage of well-trained art historians, which causes teaching departments to be understaffed or partly staffed, and keeps far below the tolerable minimum the supply of art historians to such extra-academic professions as museum curating, periodical and newspaper art criticism, and commercial dealing;

(2) the uneven distribution of well-trained art historians throughout the country, with the greatest concentration in five northeastern states. As a consequence, art departments in all other sections of the country are starved for scholars of national or international reputation.

The shortage of art historians can only be relieved by increasing the production of Ph.D.'s, and the quickest way of doing this is to give increased financial assistance to the departments of graduate study which are now the most productive (although not productive enough), i.e. the departments in the major universities in the Northeast. At the same time, however, assistance must be given to departments in the Midwest, South, and West to enable them to attract good staffs and through them good students and thus to become more effective than most of them are now in the training of professional art historians. Only by a balanced policy of support of departments in all sections of the country can the shortage of art historians be finally overcome.

The High Mortality Rate of Graduate Students in Art History

Why do so few of the many graduate students in art history eventually complete their studies, i.e. obtain the Ph.D. degree, the only meaningful degree in the field? One important reason for the high drop-out rate among art history graduate students is the insufficiency of their undergraduate training. Much of the early part of graduate work is taken up, typically, by remedial studies, designed to overcome the handicap of a spotty undergraduate training in art history and other pertinent areas, such as the languages. Many graduate students, particularly in the larger, less selective programs, spend a good deal of time in undergraduate courses. The length and laboriousness of these preliminaries discourage many. Others learn, rather late, that they have no gift for art historical work.

A high percentage of the graduate students who come to the large Eastern universities have not risen from the undergraduate programs of these schools, but have come from far away—from the Midwest, the South, the West. They represent a great variety of backgrounds and a wide range of competence. They also may reflect the provincialisms of their own original milieux. Poorly oriented, conscious of their inadequacies, torn between remedial undergraduate courses and highly specialized graduate work, overwhelmed by a sudden *embarras de richesses,* they easily become discouraged. Even those who persevere may never acquire a harmonious and coherent education in the history of art, but may go on to become one-sided and overspecialized teachers.

A major professional weakness would then seem to be an insufficient number of strong centers of undergraduate and graduate instruction throughout the country. Better departments of art in Los Angeles, Cleveland, Detroit, San Francisco, Seattle, Kansas, and Atlanta, for example, might lead to smaller, but possibly more productive, graduate programs in eastern universities. They might also promote the establishment of relatively small but possibly quite productive centers of graduate study in the various main regions of the United States.

The problems thus far mentioned are national in their scope and effect, and they are probably not wholly peculiar to art history, but rather reflect broad cultural trends which can also be observed in other fields of academic study. Dealing with them effectively will call for sweeping measures and long-range strategy. The problems to which we would like to call attention next are specific to art history and to its peculiar character and situation in America.

THE INADEQUACY OF LIBRARY RESOURCES

Several conditions combine to bring about this condition: the fairly recent arrival of art history on the American campus, with the result that earlier holdings in art history books tend to be sparse and spotty; the vastness of art historical literature, comprising publications of many centuries, none ever quite outdated, and of many countries; the scarcity and the high cost of many essential publications in art history. The need for more books was the need most frequently and most emphatically expressed to us by department chairmen. As this study has clearly demonstrated, departmental book budgets are on the whole relatively small, in many cases not sufficient to keep up with current publications, let alone with the enormous backlog of hard-to-get and out-of-print books that ought to be part of any good art historical library. Besides budgetary limitations, there exist other limiting factors, most important among them the scarcity of art librarians. Experience has shown beyond doubt that art history libraries thrive best if separately administered, i.e. if their acquisitions program is supervised by the departmental (rather than the main library) staff and if their day-by-day maintenance is in the hands of a capable art librarian. The amount of work involved in the selection, acquisition, and processing of books and in the organization and maintenance of a good art library goes beyond the capacity of all but a very few departments. Yet without such a specialized library, graduate teaching and advanced scholarship are difficult or impossible. The improvement of libraries in the history of art, is, therefore, one of the most pressing and fundamental needs. It calls for (a) substantial subsidies for library acquisition and for staff pay, and (b) a concentrated program of reprinting scarce or unobtainable books, including runs of key periodicals.

To illustrate the difficulties involved, one respondent from a western university expressed himself as follows:

My department last year spent about $16,000 for the purchase of books. This sum purchased the not very large total of about 875 titles. I estimate that the library of a department engaged in serious graduate work in the history of art should contain between 50,000 and 75,000 volumes. To attain this goal at the present rate of our spending, and assuming that the cost of books will not increase, will take us from 30 to 55 years. And this does not take into account the large yearly volume of new publications in art, in consequence of which a good art library in 30 to 55 years will require 100,000 rather than 50,000 volumes. In other words: although my book budget is actually larger than that of many other departments, I am not really making sufficient progress in building our library. In order to progress significantly, I should spend about $30,000 to $40,000 a year. But the work of selecting, ordering and processing the 2,500 to 4,000 volumes which this could buy would overtax the resources of my department and the resources of our library. It would also call for additional funds to cover the cost of processing. The only answer which I can see are large foundation grants, including sums to cover library expenses connected with the selection, classification and cataloguing of the books purchased.

The Inadequacy of Visual Aids

Our inquiries revealed that the acquisition of good slides and photographs at a reasonable cost is or should be a major concern of all art departments. With reference to slides, many department heads feel that if there were some central organization in existence for the making and distribution of slides from original photographs, the present chaotic and uneconomic system of each department making slides or ordering them from a variety of sources would happily come to an end. A committee of the College Art Association has been formed to study this whole question. The present study can only recommend that as one of the highest priorities for the long-term improvement of the teaching of history of art a non-profit educational lantern-slide center be organized.[11] This center should be sponsored by the College Art Association itself and, if administratively practical, actu-

11. For the short term, and until a national center can be organized, individual departments will need all the assistance possible for the growth and maintenance of their slide collections.

ally run by the Association with an adequate staff, including a full-time director, photographers, and file clerks or secretaries to handle orders and distribution. In 1961–62 the total slide budget for 264 departments, our questionnaire revealed, came to $172,600, to meet an annual demand of 233,000 slides. Since by no means all departments answered our questionnaire it is conservative to estimate that at least a quarter of a million dollars is being spent annually in America by art departments for slides alone. It is also a safe estimate that in the absence of a central depository of negatives from good photographs a majority of these slides are being made from bookplates with a consequent loss or distortion of detail and textural values. A well-run slide center could provide both black-and-white and color slides at a considerable reduction in unit cost and by careful control of quality of production maintain a standard of uniform excellence throughout. The procedure would be for such a center to build up an archive of master negatives on fine-grain film stock, made from original photographs in existing university and museum collections here and abroad. Even so, perhaps a majority of new photographs would have to be taken by the center's own photographers, particularly color photographs, and here the existence of a non-profit slide center would probably give access to public and private collections of art now closed to commercial photographers or available only at considerable fees, which must be passed on to the consumer. A basic service of the center might be to offer film strips of up to one thousand frames covering a particular period of art history. The department with a modest budget could then cut and mount the frames and thus reduce the total cost of individual slides by one-half or more. However, this is not the place to go into detailed costs of slides or, for that matter, the initial budget for the setting up of a lantern-slide center. Unquestionably, if the money can be found to finance such an organization from public and/or private sources the advantages for art history study would not only be economic; high quality, low-cost slides could be made available to hundreds of institutions here and abroad not now in a position to obtain them.

Good slides are important for teaching. Good photographs are essential from which to make good slides. Photographs for research purposes are another matter. Not all research photographs are useful for teaching. But the need exists for a systematic extension of photographic resources for the study of all periods of art history. Because of the vast extent of art history it is not practical to attempt to assemble under one roof a reference library of original photographs of all the world's art. Photograph collections already exist, such as those of the Italian Soprintendenze, the French Archives Photographiques, Marburg in Germany, the Courtauld Institute in London, the Frick Art Reference Library in New York, and the university collections of Harvard, Princeton, and Chicago. What would be of great value for research, and incidentally as a source for slide negatives, would be a project to reproduce in microfilm all existing photograph collections. From microfilm postcard-size reproductions would be made. Hopefully, a total file of all the postcard prints should exist in at least one institution, where it would be accessible for open consultation. The entire microfilm collection should also be kept in one place where mechanical facilities for its preservation and staff are available to make prints for circulation as widely as may be necessary. Portions of the archive of special interest to any single institution, Oriental, Medieval, Renaissance, architecture, etc., could be reproduced *en bloc*. The Museum of Modern Art, for example, might complete its already large collection of photographs of twentieth-century art, Michigan its Near Eastern collection, Harvard its Asiatic and Renaissance collections, and so on. Collection of original large photographs would continue to be the business of individual institutions, as it is now, but an enormous service would be rendered to all by the availability of an actual illustrated catalogue of all known photographic holdings, with an indication of the source of each photograph and fairly complete identifying information already on it.

Both these slide and photograph archives are expensive projects—too expensive for any one institution to finance alone. What is needed, if art history in America is to make significant progress, is that a concerted effort be made by the profession, under the aegis of the College Art Association, to secure the necessary funds from public and private donors. The major American research libraries are now among the greatest in the world. The art historian needs comparable resources in photographs and slides if his subject is to achieve the stature its extent and diversity imply.

What we are saying here, in effect, is that the tools of art history are more expensive than those in use by many other departments of the humanities. Art history is a relatively young subject. Coordination of scholarly effort is no more in evidence in it than in the other liberal arts. Unless a considerable effort is made to increase the availability of photographs and slides through the formation of central and specialized archives, art history research will remain inhibited, the province of a select few who are fortunate enough to receive research and travel assistance or who have private means.

Publication Limitations

High costs have driven from the field all general scholarly journals except *The Art Bulletin,* supported by the efforts of the whole profession, and *The Art Quarterly,* supported by private funds from the Detroit Institute of Arts (Founder's Society), the Archives of American Art, and advertising. In addition there are a few periodicals devoted to special aspects of the field: *The Journal of the Society of Architectural Historians, Ars Orientalis.* Of these the first two are sustained partly by membership, the last is financed jointly by the Freer Gallery of Art and the University of Michigan.

The publication of articles on the arts in more general cross-disciplinary periodicals (e.g. *Renaissance Studies, Victorian Studies*) is almost non-existent.

The need for illustrations of high quality, a unique problem of art historical scholarship, adds to the general high cost of printing and production. The imposed restrictions affect the amount printed, the length of articles, the number of illustrations, and also bring about a great backlog of manuscripts awaiting publication.

The Art Bulletin publishes an average of three articles and four notes per issue while receiving one and one half as many acceptable manuscripts. During the last two editorships the period between receipt and publication of manuscripts rose from twelve to eighteen or twenty-four months. *The Art Quarterly,* with its museum orientation, its interest in connoisseurship and the treatment of single objects of art, draws on a smaller number of contributors and does not impose such long delays on authors.[12]

12. Even so, the editors of *The Art Bulletin* and *The Art Quarterly* are said to be having difficulty getting manuscripts of the *quality* they need.

While the number of productive scholars in universities and museums is increasing, the number of outlets for expanding the volume of output is diminishing. And financial controls restrict the broadening of *scope;* scholarly journals cannot afford to accept technical and critical articles even when they appear to be a stimulus for the academic world.

Any attempts to economize in production such as lowering standards of paper stock and of illustrations are not only undesirable intrinsically but actually affect costs very little.

The possibility of increased circulation is slight in basic research journals, especially in the field of art history which, like musicology, is small to begin with and does not spread into secondary education.

The danger appears to be not so much that our journals shall be forced to cease publication, but that our inability to grow in pace with the growth of our field will make our publications gags rather than mouthpieces. It is possible that if competent authors had to be turned away, one would eliminate the young and inexperienced rather than the established ones, with the result that the fresh voice would be silenced; it should be given the chance to falter a bit.

Editing needs the experience, knowledge, and tact of a distinguished scholar, the sort of man who has the least time to give. The fact that editors are not paid is not crucial, but they do need much more secretarial and editorial assistance than they get.

The Art Bulletin hires a managing editor, a production expert who is needed for managing layout and controlling quality of illustration and for initial copy- and proofreading. This still leaves the chief editor menial chores of final copy- and proofreading, correspondence on minor matters with authors and readers, etc. The additional paid help of a trained historian is essential for any scholarly journal in order to leave the editor free for executive decisions and judgments; without this it will become increasingly difficult to persuade anyone to accept an editor's job.

Bulletin authors and readers are unpaid; *Quarterly* authors receive a fee. The capacity of the former to pay a token fee might attract more foreign material and would help to compensate authors for large expenditures for photographic supplies and coypright fees on photographs.

Most institutions abroad and many at home cannot afford subscriptions to major American scholarly journals in the field. A program to supply them and to initiate exchanges would benefit both the profession and the country by demonstrating our achievements at the same time as our generosity and sympathy.[13]

Recently *The Art Bulletin*—until now supported by membership dues of the College Art Association and contributions from art departments and private sources that have had to be solicited each year—has been awarded a Kress Foundation grant of $15,000 annually that will, during the brief term of the grant, cover the costs of the enlarged issues and increased staff as recommended in this report.

If these funds were to be made available over a longer period, additional funds could be spent to support a journal intended to address a larger public, playing the role of that admirable but now defunct institution, *The Magazine of Art*. As increasing numbers of art historians

13. It should be added that *Ars Orientalis* is distributed free to over twenty institutions in the United States and to over one hundred abroad.

begin to write for journals of criticism (e.g. *Art International, Arts*) it is clear that there would be a larger supply of material than there was when *The Magazine of Art* failed. The huge potential audience for intelligible writing on art is attested also by the boom in the art book market.

The College Art Association supports a series of monographs—scholarly works larger than long articles, smaller than the usual book. Its problems, of the same order, also will be temporarily alleviated by the Kress Foundation grant amounting to another $15,000 annually. The regular publication of monographs should increase circulation to libraries which can thereby subscribe as they do to serial publications.

The Association also publishes the *Art Journal,* a news medium for its membership and a journal for the exchange of ideas on contemporary art and artists, the teaching of art, and college museum problems. It carries book reviews and advertising. As a house organ it is not in competition for outside funds.

So much for periodical or monograph publications. What of the difficulties of scholarly art book publication, as distinguished from the popular picture books which flood the market? The difficulties are vividly described by one distinguished American art historian (who chooses to remain anonymous), in the following communication to our study.

It is impossible now, and never has been possible, to publish a scholarly book in our field (by which I mean a piece of original research, not what the French would call *"haute vulgarisation"*) without a substantial subsidy. This is as true of Europe as it is of America. Such books cannot pay for themselves for two reasons: because of the need for adequate illustrations, they are much more expensive to produce (and hence to buy) than scholarly books in other fields; and the total number of buyers is too small to permit editions of a size that would approach the break-even point (that point is now about 5,000 copies). Nowadays, a scholarly book in the $15–$40 range is likely to sell, in very exceptional circumstances, up to 3,000 copies (an example would be Panofsky's "Early Netherlandish Painting," of which even a slightly larger number has been sold); generally, 1,000 copies is the limit. Rock-bottom world-wide demand for more expensive books (e.g. Krautheimer's "Corpus of Early Christian Basilicas in Rome") is around 500 copies. There is, I think, only one other academic discipline that suffers from a similar handicap, and that is musicology. Those disciplines that make up the standard curriculum of American colleges (history, languages, etc.) are not only larger numerically (compare membership figures of the College Art Association with those of the Modern Language Association or the American Historical Association) but their books are cheaper to produce. Still, scholarly books in the history of art get published every year, here as well as in Europe. How is this done? In Europe, the necessary subsidies are largely provided by the State, directly or indirectly (via channels such as Max Planck Gesellschaft in Germany), while in this country there is no regular source of publication subsidies at all. A few university departments have publication funds of their own; once in a while a university press will provide its own subsidy from earnings of profit-making publications; and some foundations have subsidized a number of important scholarly books in recent years. But what is the author of a scholarly book to do if he is not lucky enough to teach at a place that has publication funds or a wealthy university press, and whose book a major foundation has refused to sponsor? He can go around shaking his tin cup in front of some of the innumerable small foundations, one or the other of which may come across with something; he can make a subsidy for his book a bargaining point if he is offered a better position by another university; or he can dip into his own pocket.

Even a casual glance at the annual production of scholarly books in the history of art here and in Europe will show that proportionately Europe produces many more than we do, despite the fact that as a nation we are richer and have roughly the same number of art historians by now. It would be fair to say that the annual production of scholarly books in our field by a single major European nation (England, France, Germany, or Italy) is roughly the same as in this country. Which means, if we regard Western Europe as a whole as roughly equal to the U.S. in population and wealth, that Europe produces three to four books when we produce one. In discussing this state of affairs with foundation officials, I have not heard anybody deny the correctness of the above estimate. But I have often been told that the reason is simple: American art historians write fewer books than Europeans. I have also often been told that "every scholarly book worth publishing is eventually published," so there really is no problem and no need to provide subsidies. This argument strikes me as of the same sort as the belief that "those who die young deserve to die young." All one can say is that if it were even more difficult to publish scholarly books in our field than it is today, even fewer books would get written and published.

The difficulties of book publication here described have been confirmed by many scholars this study has interviewed. Surely the unusual expense of illustrated art books demands more financial support than most foundations and university presses have so far seen fit to give. If periodical publication is being inhibited for lack of funds, how much more serious for the future of art scholarship are financial restrictions on the publication of book-length research in which years of a scholar's life have been invested.

Subsidized Study Travel

American teaching in art history is based on slides, books, and photographs. American scholarship in art history, insofar as it is carried on by teachers, is also largely based on books and photographs. Many American scholars carry on their work remote from original works of art, either because they are unable to get at them, or because they do not feel the need for an immediate contact with original works. The character of American teaching in the history of art has been deeply influenced by this condition, and so has the character of American scholarship, though to a lesser extent.

Since World War II, subsidized student travel has become a large-scale enterprise. Many universities support undergraduate programs abroad (Stanford, for example, has campuses in Florence, Tours, Stuttgart, Tokyo, and Taiwan, and will shortly open additional ones in Austria and England). Since these undergraduate programs are nearly always concerned with general studies or language training, art history plays only an incidental part in them. They are important for the teaching of art history nevertheless, since they bring American students by the thousands face to face with foreign art and stimulate in many an interest which otherwise would have remained dormant. Wherever such programs are offered, the effect on enrollments in art history is quite evident. It is also probable that students once exposed to great original works of art will be less likely thereafter to remain content with book study in art history.

The travel grants for graduate study which are offered by some universities, the U.S. government, some foreign governments, and a number of foundations are more directly relevant to our inquiry. Virtually every graduate student in art history spends some time in Europe, usually as the beneficiary of a program of grants. Are more grants or more extended grants needed? Most of the department chairmen we questioned insisted—some spontaneously, others upon being asked—that additional travel grants would be of great benefit to their students. Very few departments directly control travel grants. In nearly every instance, students in art history must compete with students in other areas for university or outside travel grants. What many departments desire is a subsidy to them which would enable them to send their graduate students, or at any rate the best of them, abroad more or less routinely, as a regular part of their training.

But in this connection we should remember that there is considerable pressure on art history graduate students, as there is on graduate students in general, to get the degree as soon as possible and to move on into the professional world without delay. This means that American graduate students rarely indulge in the luxury of prolonged *Wanderjahre,* unless they happen to enjoy private means which relieve them of worry about their future job. Most students feel that they ought to stick close to their department, attend the conventions, and be seen by potential employers. To disappear for several years into Europe, for independent study and self-cultivation, is something which only the most confident and independent spirits will dare to do.

The main problem appears to be not simply to get more graduate students to Europe, Africa, or Asia, but to keep them there for a sufficient length of time. Measures to be considered in this respect are:

(a) subsidies which would enable married graduate students to support their families abroad;

(b) subsidies to departments to make it easier for them to give leaves of absence to their junior staffs (i.e. to pre-doctoral instructors);

(c) the setting up of research centers in the history of art in Europe and elsewhere, jointly sponsored by various departments, to serve as bases for graduate students and regular staff. These centers would not only make life abroad easier and more economical for graduate students, but would also keep them in closer touch with their departments and the profession in general.

American academic scholars in the history of art are in somewhat the same predicament as their graduate students in the matter of foreign travel. Travel stipends are not difficult to get, though many grants are too small to support wife and children in Europe. Most travel grants must be supplemented in some way. But aside from these financial considerations, there is another obstacle to foreign travel. In the present situation of teacher shortage, it is becoming more and more difficult to cover a department's course offering. If a considerable propor-tion of teachers in art history were to absent themselves from their departments every three or four years, or even more frequently, this would very seriously aggravate the shortage and lead to drastic reductions in the course offering. Equivalent replacements for teachers on leave are already extremely difficult to find, since few teachers are tempted by brief visiting appointments. In a small department, the frequent absence of key members can produce a very serious disorganizing effect. Thus, it would be a mistake to consider the problem of travel grants without giving a great deal of attention to the problem of replacements, which is really more difficult to solve than the purely financial problem involved. It is probable that if the shortage of teachers continues, as it is likely to continue for at least some years, schools and departments will become increasingly careful about permitting leaves of absence beyond the normal sabbaticals. There is no easy remedy for this situation.

THE NEED FOR MORE TIME FOR RESEARCH AND WRITING

Although teaching loads are generally not very heavy (6 lecture-hours per week having become the standard in the better departments), it is not easy to pursue research in a university setting. The burdens of committee work and other academic obligations, of thesis supervision and counseling, and the petty administrative chores which are becoming the bane of life in the American university can cut deeply into the energy and time needed for sustained scholarly work. One reason why European professors by and large tend to be more productive than their American colleagues is, certainly, that they have more time to give to their research and writing. Time and quiet are the brain-worker's most precious allies; unfortunately, much time is wasted at American universities and much energy dissipated in busywork. Anything that might give relief from the daily distractions of university routines would be a boon to the productive art historian. Unfortunately, most of the remedies which might be tried—such as a program of short-term leaves for those in the process of undertaking or completing important scholarly work—encounter the same difficulty as expanded programs of travel grants: the prevailing shortage of teachers.

A great service could be rendered to art historians through the establishment of a specialized research institute in this country (somewhat comparable to the institutes of advanced study at Princeton and Palo Alto) dedicated to the undisturbed pursuit of research for periods of a semester, a year, or even several years. On a more modest scale, scholars could be aided by research grants which provide fairly generously for secretarial or technical help. The time and effort which go, year after year, into the clumsy typing efforts of learned men (while administrators monopolize the secretarial staffs) should be put to more productive use.

CONCLUSION: ART HISTORY IN THE ACADEMIC SETTING

American art history scholarship is still young and has only a brief history. James Ackerman, in his recent study of the profession,[14] counted only four generations of American art historians, spanning about seventy years. Is it possible to speak of a distinctly American style of art history? It is probably too early for such a determination, but a few generalizations may be hazarded nevertheless.

For one thing, American art history scholarship has been mainly based on the universities. The type of the independent, unattached scholar, the *Privatgelehrte* so relatively common in Europe, is rare in America, though there have been a few distinguished representatives of the species—Berenson, for example, who may, however, not have been sufficiently "American" to be included here. Museum-connected scholars have occasionally done excellent work—the publications of the Museum of Modern Art come to mind in this connection—but by and

14. James S. Ackerman and Rhys Carpenter: *Art and Archaeology* (The Princeton Studies, Humanistic Scholarship in America), Englewood Cliffs, N.J.: Prentice-Hall, Inc., 1963.

large the American art historian tends to be a professor.

For another thing, American art history has maintained a markedly cautious tone and conservative temper. Soundness, rather than daring or brilliance, is its chief quality. *The Art Bulletin,* surely a rock of soundness, though certainly not the most brilliant, daring, or even readable publication in its field, is its worthy and characteristic representative which faithfully reflects its temper and tone. With few exceptions, the triumphs of American art history scholarship have been won through careful workmanship and method, rather than through fresh discovery or the formulation of new ideas. Their soundness and caution, their prudent specialization, have preserved American art historians from the sweeping speculations, the doctrinaire excesses and flagrant errors to which some of their European colleagues have been prone, but they have also dampened the spirit of their students and lessened their enthusiasm, and have made them look to Europe for a periodic renewal of stimulation.

Is there a connection between the two conditions which have just been noted? There would appear to be. The preoccupation with soundness, the overemphasis on method, the caution and conservatism of American art history are university-bred qualities. They are academic qualities. Like the eclectic campus architecture which surrounds him, the American student and scholar in the humanities is profoundly conditioned by the economics of the academic marketplace and the bureaucratic patterns of university administration. From his student years onward, he passes through a succession of tests and ordeals which are designed to weed out the unsound and unacademic. The acceptance procedures of graduate programs and the hiring policies of departments, the world of committee action and deanly decree—all these are designed to smooth out irregularity and to minimize eccentricity. One wonders how Berenson would have fared in the academic business, and one knows how some other scholars of independent turn of mind have in fact fared in the groves of Academe.

The academic establishment has failed, in short, to release into society any sizeable number of productive non-university scholars in art—museum men, critics, publicists, dealers.[15] One tends to attribute this failure to the fact that the relatively few professionals who are turned out year by year are attracted most strongly by the salaries, fringe benefits, and security which universities offer, and therefore stay out of the rough and tumble of the outside world. But perhaps an additional reason is the fact that our university training produces university-minded and university-centered art historians, who by their very mentality are rendered unwilling to leave school.

15. See table 6, *Percentage of Ph.D. students graduating within the five years previous to 1961–62 who became college or university teachers.*

The Practice of Art

INTRODUCTION

The confrontation of the artist and the American campus is not a new phenomenon. The first studio-based collegiate-degree program was begun some eighty-five years ago. Before World War I, Syracuse, Yale, several state universities in the Midwest, the Carnegie Institute of Technology, Washington University (St. Louis), and many more were well along toward the assimilation of practicing artists into academic life. Many of the independent professional schools—in Philadelphia, Chicago, Boston, New York, and elsewhere—have even longer histories, of course. At some point in the early 1930s (the correlation with problems of the Great Depression is not established), the paths of the independent schools and the colleges crossed. During those years, under certification pressure from the states, and in order to compete with state college teacher preparation systems, and for various other reasons, a number of independent professional schools sought degree alliances with nearby colleges. At the same time, in increasing numbers the colleges were cautiously extending their own faculties to include practicing painters, sculptors, printmakers, and craftsmen. Some campuses, of course, had well-established studio programs in the '20s or much earlier. The schools named above were among the pioneers, but the '30s provided the climate necessary for the significant growth of many art programs in the colleges.

This proliferation of campus studio activity was not accomplished without soul searching and hesitation. The pattern of college-based studio enterprise had to sustain it neither precedent in European education nor the broad support of social belief in the artist as a valued citizen. The impulse for its inception grew out of our peculiar beliefs concerning teacher education, our respect for academic nomenclature, our academic structures, which could accommodate the change without inviting public or government strictures (as long as teacher education was the principal issue) and the example of a few pioneer colleges. The latter, in turn, owed their existence to a few enlightened individuals.[1] The colleges were not slow to see that if the independent schools could borrow from them a number of academic courses to make up a degree program, the colleges could in response add campus studio courses to the same end. For the most part, early campus offerings were presented within a liberal arts framework, with the Bachelor of Arts degree as terminus. Studio performance was kept at a genteel "cultural enlightenment" level. But more utilitarian programs also existed based on needs developed in departments of home economics, architecture, engineering, and classics, all of which used drawing as a descriptive or expressive tool. Artists of quality and consequence did emerge from these submerged professional programs; but to some extent full acceptance of responsibility for the education of artists came gradually and as a result of complex forces, and faculties which might have been apprehensive about assigning college credit for courses in which the hand as well as the mind played a part were not always immediately aware of the intrusion, at least not to the point of insisting on a strict academic rationale for the event. The need for teacher preparation courses in art was a sufficient first cause in many instances, and indeed the teachers colleges housed at the outset some of the most strongly studio-oriented campus programs.

1. John Ferguson Weir, for example, who became the first director of the Yale School of the Fine Arts in 1869, and George Fisk Comfort, who was active in the organization of the College of Fine Arts at Syracuse in 1873.

The transition from the business of training art teachers to the recruitment of practicing artists on faculties was not a particularly intricate maneuver. The inclusion of painters and sculptors on faculty lists came quietly—and early appointments tended to be conservative, obligating the colleges to no point of view that could not be sustained by the academic tradition. Also, for the most part, an interest in studio offerings, except for those students who came to the colleges to prepare for primary and secondary school teaching, tended to be superficial if not frivolous. There were, however, a few institutions—including those already named—which early made strong commitments to the serious teaching and practice of art. These adopted liberal faculty recruitment policies, made special space available for painters, sculptors, and craftsmen, and evolved a balanced curriculum, including both studio and non-studio courses. The terminal degree of such campus-based programs was that of Bachelor of Painting or Bachelor of Fine Arts. Except for the giving of degrees, these early college programs were very similar to those of the independent art schools.

Since the 1920s, and particularly in the last twenty years, the growth of studio departments in American colleges has been phenomenal. An index of this stupendous growth is to be found in the following totals of institutions offering a graduate program in studio work and the number of graduate degree candidates enrolled. These figures are in response to a questionnaire sent to 264 institutions (a majority of colleges did not offer a graduate degree in studio work).

	1940–41	1950–51	1960–61
Number of institutions responding	11	32	72
Total candidates	60	320	1,365

Some further figures. In 1961 the total *undergraduate* enrollment in studio courses (197 institutions responding) was 43,115. The total enrollment in graduate studio courses in 1961 (58 institutions responding) was 2,862. Obviously many undergraduate courses in studio work are taken by students who either do not, or find they cannot, go on to graduate study. Nevertheless, the postwar increase in the number of those who profess to be professionally dedicated art students is staggering. With these statistics in mind the present study has chosen to concentrate on the following aspects of the subject: art education before college; art as a profession and art as a handmaiden of the liberal arts; the support of studio courses by college administrations; the campus environment and the art student; the independent school versus the college in the preparation of artists; the artist-teacher on the campus; the academic degree as a measure of artistic excellence; the studio program and history of art; and, finally, accreditation procedures.

Pre-College Art Education

Generally speaking, attempts by the colleges to attract talented art students are low keyed. In contrast to the independent professional schools which advertise vigorously or make positive efforts to recruit talent, the colleges tend to accept what comes to them. There is, to be sure, some participation in College Day and similar programs. Some colleges use traveling exhibits, some have summer camp or summer school activity to keep the pot boiling. But with pressure for admission growing, colleges tend to let nature take its course, bringing in as much talent on each tide of new students as it will. A sufficient quantity of students at the entrance level will feed the selection process as general students develop into art majors at the second-year, third-year, or graduate levels. No college will admit to being shortchanged on talent. The assumption generally is that a school will attract talent if its reputation is favorably known.

Coupled with the foregoing is a general consensus that art education at the primary and secondary levels is inadequate, if we are to apply as a measure either the awakening of artistic sensibility or balanced awareness of the social and economic implications, not to mention the technical ones, of an artist's life. As elements of general education, on the other hand, and in the interests of students who are untalented or unaware of talent, the arts appear to have been assigned an insignificant role at secondary levels. All schools interviewed can cite exceptions to these circumstances, but state with great positiveness that art is on the whole inadequately taught at pre-college levels. Good high school art teaching when it exists is more apt to be present in city schools than in the towns.

Thus the development of a general response to the visual arts becomes by default the responsibility of the colleges. If a student is to be awakened to art, he must wait for a college or an independent school to do the job. Some students who demonstrate talent at an early age choose to go to an independent school, either because they are anxious to test their professional capabilities as directly and as rigorously as they can or because of their unwillingness to become involved in the more diversified teaching programs which characterize many colleges. Other students with sufficient intellectual capactiy to handle college work or to meet institutional entrance requirements, at least, and who may have had to submit to

strong parental pressure, gravitate toward colleges because they or their parents are suspicious of "vocational"
education. If they have talent, if they are sufficiently well
guided, and if they are fortunate enough to discover a
professional studio atmosphere in which to develop, the
chances that they can progress at a rate equal to or faster
than that of their independent art school fellows is good.
For those students who clearly can benefit from specific
education in areas of painting, sculpture, or design, the
inclination of the colleges has been to emulate, when they
have had the capacity to do so, the intricate procedures
which the independent academies have long employed in
their development of artists. If the campus has inadequate
facilities for the full development of talent only waste
ensues.

The majority of college art department heads and faculty we have interviewed voice dissatisfaction with the
quality of art teachers in the secondary schools, though
some believe that the situation is improving. Curiously
enough, most colleges feel little responsibility for the
state of pre-college art education. Some, however, con-
ceded that they might have to take more aggressive action
toward solving problems related to teaching at pre-college levels. There were various views as to how this should
be done. A number indicated that the proper place to
begin an improvement program might be by the institution of special graduate programs in art teacher education. Another quite logical enterprise might be based on
higher studio standards for those preparing to teach art,
their more imaginative preparation in areas of perceptual
awareness, more mature demands in research-oriented
programs, more consequential innovations in technical
means, more effective projection of the arts as indispens-
able ingredients of a good—and certainly of a great—

society. All this preparation may take longer than the orthodox four undergraduate years. This may also imply more careful selection of the people who apply as postulant teachers. It certainly suggests that all schools professing to have capability for art teacher education be equipped to teach the visual arts as a significant human response, not one requiring apology or deserving of only casual attention, but generative, disciplined in particular ways, demanding, exciting, and capable of far-reaching development.

Current certification agencies for pre-college teachers were generally criticized because of their lack of insistence on adequate studio experience for art teachers, and for their willingness to accept theory as a substitute for content. Also the extent to which some states extend a teacher's responsibility to the coverage of any subject in the curriculum (without regard to his preparation) has nullified in significant ways the meaning of certification. This we found notably true in California. Certification practices of this indiscriminate kind result in the appointment of qualified art teachers as, for example, mathematics instructors; conversely mathematics teachers often end up teaching art classes. It does not seem that this method is designed to produce the best results either for artists or for mathematicians.

In the opinion of most college department heads, and confirming the opinions stated above, the studio course content required for pre-college teacher certification by the various states is considered to be too low. College art departments want more studio preparation for teachers, more courses in the humanities in their programs, more practice teaching. There is a notable impatience with courses required by departments of education, along with a desire to see art education proceed in "depth" toward competence in something—design, painting, sculpture, crafts, or whatever.

Flexibility in the matter of teacher certification was generally held desirable, though "flexibility" was variously interpreted. Most respondents thought that the constraints imposed by certifying agencies, when not downright stultifying, at best inhibited experimentation and supported mediocre schools. That outstanding students are not being attracted to secondary school teaching as a profession can be assigned, in part at least, to the imposition of state-mandated programs. Most colleges we interviewed felt that responsibility for teacher certification ought to be within the jurisdiction of the colleges themselves where it could be best controlled, rather than by either state offices or the National Council for Accreditation of Teacher Education. It was held that if they set their own standards the colleges will soon be sorted out on the basis of quality of the preparation they give rather than on any other considerations. Few who discussed the matter are willing to assign the responsibility for teacher certification beyond state levels.

The deficiencies of students coming into the colleges from high schools are a matter of concern to both art teachers and administrators. The majority of those interviewed were disturbed by the average high school student's undeveloped awareness and consequent lack of respect for the disciplines of art. It would appear that, in the view of the colleges, art training at the secondary school level is far too permissive and superficial. One college administrator commented that the high schools tend to encourage dispersion of activity rather than depth of experience of any kind. Highly specialized work should not be the goal of any high school class, but it is possible, under proper guidance at the high school level, to do more than sample techniques. Lack of any kind of preparation in art history at the high school level was also cited as a major weakness. The opinion was general that, for the most part, secondary school training is of little consequence when students move into college art classes, and that differences in high school preparation tend to disappear once students have embarked on the more systematic studio experience provided in serious campus programs.

So-called commercial art courses in high schools are considered by most college teachers to be not only inadequate but positively dangerous, as they tend to give students a formulated and therefore false notion of what constitutes a professional solution to visual problems.

Drawing as it is handled on the high school level is generally acknowledged to be weak. There is no single pattern of inadequacy in drawing preparation. Administrators variously commented on it as being too conservative, or too strongly dominated by technique, or too loosely expressive. One experienced administrator spoke of "conceptual weakness" on the part of students coming to him from the schools. Another said of incoming students, "we have to redesign them almost completely." The problem of drawing was constantly referred to as one no longer handled adequately at pre-college level. The strongest students appear to be those who have had some contact with original works of art and have gained a certain amount of sophistication through their use of gallery and museum resources. Students tend to do best in college when they have been pushed both technically and intellectually while still in secondary schools.

The lack of high school teachers who are fully informed specialists and who can give wise guidance to young and aspiring art students is of course at the bottom of most of such difficulties. With little awareness themselves of our cultural heritage, teachers with limited experience and understanding can impart only the most meager concepts to their students. Such teachers tend to have little identification with art as an active force and their students reflect this lack of involvement in the creative process.

Some colleges attribute the problem of pre-college art teaching to the cultural climate of our times. The common lack of understanding of what art is and how it functions in society, the disciplines it requires, and the qualities of imagination and resourcefulness it demands of its best practitioners has its effect on the judgment of even those we call our best-educated citizens. There was such depressing unanimity of opinion among those we interviewed that it would almost seem that the teaching of art in most high schools is detached from reality altogether. In many places art teaching has no particular function of its own and does not lead effectively into advanced work.

To repeat, however, it should be more apparent than it is to the colleges that a share of the responsibility for this condition is their own. They cannot hope to expect better students from the high schools unless they provide better instruction for those who are going to teach high school students.

All public and some private colleges formally acknowledge their responsibility for teacher education.[2] Most

2. This responsibility is shared by a great many excellent unaffiliated professional schools, of course. Notable programs in art teacher education have been a part of teaching responsibility in such excellent schools as the School of the Art Institute of Chicago, the Rhode Island School of Design, and the Massachusetts College of Art, among others, for many years. These and other professional schools have prepared significant numbers of superior teachers.

studio faculties, however, view this responsibility with mixed enthusiasm, especially when control of courses in methodology is largely out of their hands. Studio courses tend, under these conditions, to become service courses for schools or departments of education, sometimes dominating and sometimes being dominated by education faculties in curricular matters. As controls by art faculties increase, there tends to be more interest on the part of studio teachers in the education of embryo pre-college teachers. When the responsibility is not entirely theirs, they more often than not complain of their obligation toward secondary school education, and this attitude results in neglect of critical areas in the preparation of teachers for such schools.

PROFESSIONAL VERSUS LIBERAL ARTS ORIENTATION

In spite of their accommodation of artists on their faculties, some colleges are reluctant to claim any responsibility for the preparation of practicing artists. The traditional liberal arts values are widely held to be those which are most important. This official view, stated by most of the administrators interviewed, was sometimes contradicted by faculty members themselves. It is extremely unlikely that an artist of first rank who finds himself on a college faculty will neglect to regard it as his responsibility to nourish any talent he may discover in a student. In the process of this nourishment, it is almost inevitable that some of the instructor's professional attitudes will influence the student, to the advantage of both. One college art department, which professed to have an interest only in contributing to a general program of liberal arts education, also spoke with pride of the opportunities its students had of getting their work into professional exhibitions. There is a puzzling confusion of professional and non-professional objectives in this case and in others. It would appear that some schools are reluctant to acknowledge the liberalizing influence of art itself, and the identification of the goals of the practicing artists with those of the humanists. The largest and most professional studio-oriented departments find it difficult to accommodate this division of interest at advanced study levels and declare themselves to be essentially on the side of those students who wish to achieve status as practicing artists. On some campuses, splinter art activities are to be found in departments of home economics, architecture, education, or one of a number of liberal arts departments; this practice sometimes permits double or triple standards to exist on a single campus. Occasionally one finds a department divided against itself, with design activity separated from painting and sculpture. Such schisms appear to have a debilitating effect on the fabric of professional studio education when carried to some of the extremes noted.

ADMINISTRATION SUPPORT OF STUDIO COURSES

It is not surprising to find enthusiasm for campus-based art programs at the general administrative level. Having established its respectability among other academic disciplines, art has been enthusiastically embraced by presidents, deans, provosts, and other top administrative officers. In view of the long neglect which once characterized art programs on most college campuses, it is a little surprising to find that the enthusiasm for them has reached, in these latter years, such a peak. It would appear that the energy inherent in the arts has been surviving on the campuses for a long time, with or without significant administrative support; now that it has broken through the crust of academic suspicion, it has erupted with spectacular force. It is true that increasingly the arts have developed a strong public appeal and this in turn has undoubtedly had its effect on administrators. It is not altogether clear whether the growth of college interest in the arts has been responsible for an increased awareness of them on the part of the public or whether public enthusiasm, for whatever reasons, has forced the arts to the attention of the colleges. At any rate, a society which has for long given lavish support to scientific, medical, and even musical activities on the campus, now accepts the visual arts as deserving of similar liberality.

In view of this enthusiasm for art on the part of college administrators, many art department heads feel that, while they have been provided with generous space and equipment with which to work, salaries in their departments are not competitive with the highest salaries on the campus. In matters of space and equipment, of course, many variables have been noted. Some schools have splendid new facilities, others work against tremendous difficulties in quarters which are totally obsolete for the purposes they are called upon to serve. There is an almost universal need for more space for graduate students (or perhaps for fewer students). In general, studio practitioners are not exempted from the general benefits which accrue to faculty members in other areas.

Liberal administrative policies, however, can be noted in a large number of institutions. Faculty efforts in creative directions are supported through research grants, through faculty leaves, and in a few cases, through favorable teaching schedules. The practice of supplying faculty studios conveniently near teaching areas is not wide-spread, but when it exists it appears to be not only greatly appreciated but productively used. A few schools also supply faculty members with the materials of their craft. This, however, is relatively rare. Exhibition costs incurred by faculty members are defrayed by a very small number of schools.

The independent art schools—many of which are capable of offering extremely good facilities, first-rate faculty, comparable programs, and stimulating supporting activities—are not presently in command of sufficient resources to meet advancing salary scale demands, the pressures of increasing fringe benefits, or the other costs of direct competition with prosperous state-supported or well-endowed private colleges, including the expansion of programs in the humanities. For the most part museum directors and boards find museum development more compatible with their interests than school development. They have not, in consequence, always responded effectively to the manifest trend toward assumption of art education responsibility by the colleges.

Faculties in the arts do not yet enjoy, on most private and some public college campuses, parity salary scales vis-à-vis their colleagues in other departments, especially those in the sciences. But the differences in opportunity to earn a satisfactory wage and to qualify for concomitant benefits are even greater between campus and independent schools. Justification for this assertion is to be found in a recent independent survey of representative schools in all categories.[3] Thus artists are providing subsidy for education to a significant degree. This circumstance

3. Questionnaire circulated to members of the National Association of Schools of Art, 1964–65. Of the 33 schools reporting, 16 are independent, 17 are parts of diversified educational institutions.

should be acknowledged as a real contribution to the arts and to education, by both administrators and their constituencies.

THE CAMPUS ENVIRONMENT AND THE ART STUDENT

One of the key questions asked in the interrogation of administrative officers in studio programs was: "In your opinion does the liberal arts environment offer the best hope for the preparation of artists?" The response was mixed. Those on the negative side stated that too much time is spent on extracurricular activities on the campus, and that these interfere with work in the studio. On the positive side, many administrators felt that the colleges have an advantage over most of the independent art schools, for in addition to the lure of degrees, they can provide generous scholarship support, access to the community of scholars, and participation in the cultural life of the college. These are, to be sure, formidable advantages, if used. Library resources, the stimulus of other disciplines (if these can be made useful to young artists), the regulation of student living habits, and the range of experiences which some of the independent schools are indifferent to, or entirely lack—all these favor art education on the campus. On the other hand, the pressures which academic life impose on art students and teachers are not inconsiderable. The attitude that making art is less important than discussing art still prevails on a number of campuses. If, as some administrators assert, the artist needs the intellectual environment of the college in which to mature, then the artist must resolve the dilemma which confronts him through his participation in the academic event. Hospitality to the idea of art, coupled with hostility to all the messy practices through which art comes into being, produces a sharp cleavage which no amount of adroit verbalizing can ever completely repair. The most healthy campuses, in terms of the artist's survival as teacher or student, are those which wholeheartedly accept all of the apparent confusions of art along with its graceful fruits.

THE INDEPENDENT SCHOOL VERSUS THE COLLEGE IN THE PREPARATION OF ARTISTS

What about the relative usefulness of the independent schools and the colleges when it comes to preparing artists?

The noncommittal responses to this question were that all types of schools are needed, each has its function, and each its strengths. For some students, it was felt, the academic environment provides tremendous stimulus, for others it is a distraction and delays their development as artists. However, the belief is general that the trend toward campus-based studio education is too strong to be changed and that in the future the attraction of artists to the campuses—both as teachers and as students—will increase rather than diminish. In effect, there are not simply two basic patterns of art education operating in this country, those in independent schools and those in college art departments, but a third as well: the professionally dedicated school, for example Yale, Washington University (St. Louis), the Carnegie Institute of Technology, Pratt Institute, where the values of liberal education, while present, do not dominate, where campuses enclose without confining, and where faculty members can function as artists, both in their classrooms and as part of the texture of urban life.

It is possible to get almost as many opinions concerning the need of the artist for liberal education as there are artists in the schools. Most administrators are, not unnaturally, quite loyal adherents to the party line of the colleges, which is that, of course, the artist needs a liberal education in order to be a good artist. This opinion is not stated with so much assurance by representatives of schools which have achieved strong professional programs. Here judgments seldom proceed beyond the admission that the humanities are, of course, a "good thing." There is the uncomfortable feeling in the minds of some college art school administrators that campus education for the artist should not become too regimented; what the artist really needs is opportunity to explore many avenues of interest of which humanistic studies represent only a part. Some of the chief proponents of a liberal education for artists, when confronted by another question—"What schools are the source of the best artists?"—named independent art schools. This apparent inconsistency is significant. If, indeed, the colleges are to compete with independent schools as a training ground for artists, then they must provide the climate that will produce artists. If the humanities can be justified as part of this process, well and good. If the humanities are included only as a gesture toward the academic environment in which the schools find themselves, the progress of the art student's development is likely to be delayed, if not compromised. Under such conditions the enterprising student will seek out a school where the arts are given clear priority, where the various disciplines of art are intensively pursued and where works of art have been accumulated in significant quantities. If these conditions can be met on a college campus, then the college is, in a real sense, providing professional education. One respondent noted that the great emphasis in the colleges on reading, and the priorities given generally to verbal learning, succeed only in blunting visual acuity. This accusation is coupled with a haunting belief that the university is geared to degree granting and to making the processes of education painless. The contention is that the arts cannot be mastered without pain, and that the tendency in some universities and colleges to treat the processes of technical education in the arts as theoretical and historical phenomena is irrelevant to the preparation of artists. Whatever validity this argument may have, some college administrators expressed regret that the colleges are slipping into the same patterns as the independent art schools and that the independent schools are copying the colleges. It is possible to conclude from all this uncertainty of direction that there is virtue in having a wide variety of educational patterns in the arts. But in the student's interest it would seem that the only honest procedure would be for each school to define its teaching objectives more closely than is now done so that prospective students will have no difficulty in choosing the kind of program that suits their needs.

It would be singularly unfortunate if independent art schools of quality were to dry up because of inadequate resources and, in consequence, be forced to abdicate their position in favor of either campus-based art education or out-and-out trade school activity. The strength of American art education does not lie in the independent art schools alone, or in the college humanities-oriented programs, or in the campus-based professional schools. The opportunities for experimentation, development, and effective change in the education of young artists come from the composite relationships of all these groups. The best chance we have for developing sound art education practices in this country will grow out of the nurturing of all these forces. We should face the realization that no single pattern best suits the needs of all students and, further, that variegation in the means of education will lead to variety in the result. Having gone off the academic gold standard, we are now in a free market in which rapid and strong fluctuations can be expected but out of which new values will emerge and a kind of composite standard will be set. No energetic and honest school, under whatever auspices it operates, need fear this type of change. The arts today are in a turbulent but happy state. It would be surprising and unhealthy if the schools were not deeply involved in a quest for methodology as well as for direction.

The great weakness in the position of the artist vis-à-vis his society is in the management of his product as a commodity. As he succeeds in finding a market, he becomes to a degree trapped by his success and if his product goes out of fashion he suffers in consequence. Contemporary assessment of his product fluctuates in response to many factors—exhibition acceptance, the vagaries of jury tastes, gallery promotion, museum approbation, unpredictable patterns of patronage. The arguments against formalized means of support are clear. Official patronage has too often meant control and the control is not one which inevitably concerns quality. Caught in the many cross currents of American art activity, the schools have reacted in various ways. Some of course keep to the main stream of conservative thought, following practices which have in the past produced artists (sometimes in spite of themselves), though in only a few cases have these practices been kept intact. Even with modification of method, some schools reflect the more conservative trends of the nineteenth century. Others have precisely followed, or attempted to follow, the current mode of professional activity. (They have hopped from pop to op with the greatest of ease.) Between these two extremes lies the great respectable and responsible majority of the schools. In these schools, both on and away from complex campuses, there is a search, not always successful but generally vigorous and honest, for ways to educate artists and to prepare them for the confrontations which await them: the confrontation with systems like those developing out of the Bauhaus and Ulm, the confrontation with problems of utilization—the production of objects or services for society's use—the confrontation with the problems of living and the development of attitudes consonant with today's realities, the confrontation with changing social structures, political ideologies, religious faiths, and expressive modes. The problem of art education for today's world is not simple. No single school meets all the exigencies of its position with uniform success.

THE ARTIST-TEACHER ON THE CAMPUS

What about the artists themselves who are brought to the campus? What effect does it have on their work as artists? These questions elicited a number of widely varied responses. Generally speaking, our respondents indicated, there is probably no "best" environment for the artist. If he has competence, a desire to teach, and some teaching ability, he can make a home for himself in almost any school. The correlation between sustained artistic activity and active involvement in campus life does not appear to be very great. Some artists thrive on the academic diet, others shun all associations except those most immediately concerned with art. Separation from New York and other large centers has produced in some faculty artists a sense of isolation, resulting in artistic inertia. Sometimes the security of campus routine has been beneficial, and again it has had no effect whatever on creative production. The artistically qualified may indeed be immune to sensations identified with academic life. Some have found that the campus has no appeal, and have left to cultivate other interests.

Respondents were unanimous, however, in their belief that a city environment is of tremendous advantage to the majority of creative people. The artist who finds himself in a college far removed from a metropolitan center must depend on the campus community itself for the multiple stimuli which a city provides. Here the independent professional schools, which have always been based in metropolitan centers, many times within the ambiance of distinguished museums as well, have a clear advantage. In short, no matter what its other attributes may be, a college that cannot adequately sustain the artist's interest, his productivity, and his search for expression, will tend to preserve on its faculty only those whose interests are predominantly academic rather than creative.

Many artists whose names recur on current exhibition lists tend to denigrate the effects of formal art study on their own development as artists. It is not possible to conclude from this that they are opposed to formal study, for they themselves are among those who now teach in the schools. It might be more exact to say that by becoming teachers they are attempting to find better ways to deal with the complexities of art education than those they experienced, and in this respect their discontent, doubts, and efforts at reappraisal can only mean, one would suppose, that the future will produce more results (that is, enlightened artists) than the past.

Of those who do acknowledge the influence of art schools in their lives, many report their educational influences as deriving from individual teachers—John Norton, Hans Hofmann, or the many individual artists who have been associated at one time or another with the Art Students League of New York.

Of the rest, as might be expected, many have had in their backgrounds such schools as the School of the Art Institute of Chicago, the California School of Fine Arts, the Pennsylvania Academy, the National Academy of Design, the California College of Arts and Crafts, and Pratt Institute. Yale, Cooper Union, the Rhode Island School of Design, Iowa, Syracuse, Maryland Institute, and a host of other schools, large, small, well known and obscure, have contributed to the total of significant artists of the postwar decades.

Two observations can be made as a result of our examination of the educational records of artists whose works are nationally exhibited: First, the major source of educational influence in this group has been the schools which are avowedly professional in nature, whether independent or college-affiliated. Generalized education, in which art is not taught as a professional objective, has indeed produced artists of quality. Harvard, Princeton, Reed, Stanford, Bennington, among many other liberal arts colleges, can claim such artists among their graduates. But the clearest influences have been the professional schools—a mixture of schools, or schools and individual teachers, or foreign added to American institutions. In sum, professional education can claim clear responsibility for most of the vitality of our current artistic life.

Second, as painting and sculpture depend less and less on stabilized traditional techniques, and the term "art" becomes correspondingly less restrictive as an evaluative term, the function of education for the "pure" artist, in a traditional sense, becomes increasingly less capable of precise definition. As the schools have responded—and contributed—to the demarcation of these new and more permissive limits of art, they have been confronted by the possibility that they may in the process be contributing to their own destruction.

THE ACADEMIC DEGREE

The Master's degree is almost universally accepted as the terminal degree in studio programs.[4] There is considerable opposition on the part of many of the most professional college departments toward any move which would make the doctorate in studio work a legitimate goal. Most schools consider it wasteful of talent to spend time on getting a degree beyond the Master's at the expense of one's development as an artist. Although a very few schools are trying to force the issue by awarding the doctorate, hoping thereby to gain a certain advantage for their students in the matter of preferment for faculty positions, the tide of enlightened opinion generally is against this practice.[5] Furthermore, as a measure of artistic excellence, most college department spokesmen seem to have little regard for any academic degree, as such. They do not use it as a device for measuring the competence of prospective faculty members. They do not

4. See table 9, *Number of M.F.A. degrees awarded, 1930–62.*
5. See "The Present Status of the M.F.A. Degree, A Report to the Midwest College Art Conference," *Art Journal,* XXIV, 3 (Spring 1965), 244–49.

believe that it looms very large in the evaluation of an artist, and they are convinced that it is irrelevant to all except those within the academic community who have been trained to recognize in the degree a significant measure of academic stature. Along with this repudiation of the degree as a measuring device is the reluctant acknowledgment of its usefulness as a credential when artistically unsophisticated administrators have to be impressed, and also of its increasing use as a qualifying measure in the processes of state certification for teaching. Nevertheless, as both colleges and independent art schools continue to award degrees they tend to exclude from the academic market those who have been prepared for their artistic vocations in less formal ways.

It would be unfortunate indeed if the more enlightened schools were to be persuaded by academic pressures beyond their own control that there is a correlation between the number of degree holders on art faculties and the excellence of the schools. Presidents of colleges are preoccupied with many problems; the degree may reflect for them standards which are current in other disciplines. But degrees in art have no ultimate value in the assessment of artistic competence. The quality of the school in which the degree has been earned is a better index to its value, but even that measure is unreliable. Lacking themselves the special knowledge required of those who administer art schools and departments, college administrators had better leave judgments of this kind to specialists and regard the degree credential as simply acknowledgment of an academic association with enlightened people for a mandated period. To give the degree more value than this for the artist is to run the risk of making the degree, to a greater extent than it already is, an end in itself. No student is a finished artist because of a degree, and most students, even the best of them, require a long period of maturation after their formal art studies have ended before they can lay claim to the proud title of artist. Lacking the power to assess our contemporaries as well as history will assess them, we must depend on the kinds of experience that long observation and genuine concern for the arts will supply. To believe in the degree as a sole measure of competence is the judgment of those who are more blind than they ought to be to all the complexities of an artist's nature. The degree for the artist, at best, is a by-product rather than a goal. If it impresses family, friends, and those in official places, it can hardly be considered inconsequential. But measured against all the other considerations which go to make up the judgment of an artist and his work, a degree in art is a sign of virtue rather than a real gauge of creative worth.[6]

THE STUDIO PROGRAM AND THE HISTORY OF ART

The relation of the history of art to studio courses is generally acknowledged to be an important link in the process of education. Few schools, independent or campus-based, have not paid some attention to the history of art as a part of every student's preparation. The balance between history and studio work appears to be best in those schools where administratively there exists a close bond between these two activities. If the history of art is a dominant department, then studio courses are likely to suffer through lack of adequate service in the historical studies required of their students and in the

6. See table 10, *Career choices for recipients of M.F.A. degrees, within five years previous to 1961–62.*

qualified acceptance of studio faculty members into the intellectual life of the campus. On some campuses the cleavage between history of art and studio programs is wide and deep. It would appear that some faculties are scarcely acquainted with what goes on in their sister departments.

Of all the "academic subjects" certainly history of art is the one which should be closest to those who expect to become practitioners. If properly taught to young artists, it should be a stimulus to their own effort and a means through which they can reach out to other fascinating areas of intellectual enterprise—not only to adjacent arts, but into the related realms of creative writing, history, literature, anthropology, archaeology, ethnology, and languages. It is probably a fact that this consummation is devoutly wished for more often than it is achieved. Our observation is that the history of art elicits too shallow a response from the student artists in many schools. History for the art student seems to enjoy its best chance of success when the subject is taught by someone who is himself an artist as well as an historian and who can make lively, for art students, the solutions to problems which artists of every generation, both in historical time and in our day, have found important.

ACCREDITATION PROCEDURES

Although most schools appear to believe that some clarification of standards in art education is desirable, most were uncertain about the best means to achieve this goal. The word "accreditation" was frightening to some, who regard any move toward the accreditation of an art program as a move toward bondage, which indeed under some auspices it might very well be. Both member and non-member schools in some quantity mentioned the National Association of Schools of Art as the best repository for whatever hopes they have of clarifying educational objectives across the country. The fact that accreditation does not mean standardization is not widely understood. Departments which are part of large, complex institutions have been able to avoid involvement with accreditation procedures in the arts because they have enjoyed the umbrella protection of their parent institutions. The independent schools have had no such protection and have had to work hard to achieve the kind of status which would bring them up to parity with the colleges in matters related more to economics and politics than to art, beginning with inclusion on government lists after World War II for training under the G.I. Bill; or perhaps even before that, when problems of art teacher education, curriculum acceptance by state agencies, and teacher certification required them to modify their patterns in order to survive.

CONCLUSIONS

We are moving rapidly toward the completion of an academic cycle in the teaching of art, the total effect of which is still undetermined. As colleges impose their compound influences on artists, educating them to meet the demands made by society's new awareness of art, the academic process conditions the end product in new and important ways. In one sense, there is safety for the arts in the diversity of influences at work—Bauhaus, expressionism, neo-realism, assemblage, illusionism, and many others. But, in spite of this diversity, there is often a quick transfer from idea to dogma in campus art education. The perpetuation of faculties alone (through the protec-

tive devices of tenure among other things) assures con-
tinuity of academic attitudes.

The cycle begins thus: the art student is introduced to
the academic milieu and accepts it as the natural habitat
of the artist. He grows to technical and philosophical
maturity with the campus as the center of his intellectual
and emotional world. He is conditioned by the multiform
activity around him: the academic microcosm which con-
centrates and intensifies concepts of research, the values
of verbal intercourse, the logic of scientific procedure, the
stimulus of generalized activity—athletics, fraternity life,
organizations, seminars, symposia, forums. All of these
conditions, developed to educate the "whole" student,
may in fact be helpful in producing "whole" artists. But
there are other considerations: if art education becomes
not a quest but a ritualistic part of educational life, if
artists are more confined than nurtured by humanistic
learning, if the practice of art itself in some quantity is
not made an important ingredient in an artist's perceptual
makeup, then the inevitable course of the cycle moves
toward the production of graduates who are respectable
but uninspired.

Emerging with a degree our young artist confronts a
society which offers him a choice of either "going it
alone," with all the hazards this implies, or associating
himself with some kind of institutional life. For many
aspiring "pure" artists, the greatest hope for maintaining
purity is through teaching, and thus the graduate studios
—again largely on the campuses—become a logical next
step. Out of the graduate programs, year by year, come
increasing numbers of artists thoroughly conditioned to
life in academe. They are ready and anxious to lead others
into this splendid grove, where alone, they are increas-

ingly persuaded, art hangs on the golden bough. All this despite the fact that our interviews have revealed that the annual production of would-be artist-teachers far exceeds the number of positions available at the college level.

In the educational cycle described above it is entirely possible that the values of art are somehow merged with the values of learning as a discrete activity. Art can thus be conditioned by the intellectual life and become itself intellectualized. It is made to appear more real through verbal description than in the fact of its own existence. It is embraced by the academic establishment. It becomes in a real sense official, though its variance from the forms of an earlier academy may be marked. Innovation for the sake of innovation may, in fact, be its academic hall-mark.

It is apparent that serious and thoughtful artists in some quantity are teaching art in the colleges. Their belief in the opportunity afforded in campus studios for the encouragement and development of art and artists is documented by their words and by their work. The careful attention given to studio instruction in college art departments which do not hesitate to call themselves "professional" should not be confused with the restricted influence, even obscurity, which characterizes some small art departments submerged in a vast complex of other departments of learning. The worst thing, in our view, that can happen to an artist or an art department is to be the object of polite tolerance. It is better to be loved or hated. In spite of a growing realization in society at large that art has singular importance, there persists a belief in some colleges that the arts must take on the protective coloration of scholarship if they are to be tolerated in the midst of scholarly enterprises. It is this urge toward

conformity, in people and in programs, that may defeat
the aims of art in the end, at least as these aims are
manifested in the colleges.

It is clear that art, in spite of its increasingly popular
appeal, is still an underground movement as far as secondary school education is concerned. The colleges, it
would appear, have prepared insufficient numbers of
capable, discerning artist-teachers for the high schools,
and must share with other agencies some responsibility
for the dearth of good teaching in secondary schools.

It is understandable that the current flood of publications, reproductions, exhibitions, and critical comment,
and the excitement which accompanies every excursion
into new modes of expression should have a massive
impact on students, introducing them early to the glam-
our of professional success. Unfortunately, many students
are encouraged by the unpredictability of the marketplace to develop an easy confidence in their own competitive strength. Here lies the greatest danger to budding
talent. We are not making sufficient distinction between
art as an inscrutable, private expression, without limits,
uncontrolled and unassessable—and in these terms un-
teachable—and art as a search for meaning in somewhat
larger terms, a search that involves internal disciplines
of mind and spirit as well as the acknowledgment of
technical controls. If there is no search, if there are no
limits, if art is completely free both at the beginning and
at the end of the educational experience, as well as at all
the stages in between, then it would appear that art has
no place among the academic disciplines. It would be
equally true to say that an educational process that re-
stricts itself to technical training alone is dull and un-
rewarding.

Education in the arts must lie somewhere between

exaltation of natural impulse and subservience to technical method. In the best schools, both on and off the campus, a balance is achieved. But other schools tend strongly toward one extreme or the other with educational aims either never clearly defined, or fluctuating from one faculty member to the next. The central issues of art education need clarification if they are to be properly discussed. Art is not a private world once its evolution in the presence of the artist has ceased. It becomes public and vulnerable. Its defense lies only in its own being; its values are the values people bring to it. There are good reasons to project the problems of art into a broader context than that supplied by art teachers and students alone. Departments of art, having arrived on campus with confidence in their mission to educate broadly, and having been brought by virtue of their signal successes to a point where professional training is also their acknowledged or tacit concern, should now examine with dispassionate care the whole range of their responsibilities: toward education in general through introduction (or reintroduction) of visual experience to as many students as may wish to enlarge their understanding of the world in this dimension; toward the history of art, their closest ally (and sometimes most suspicious critic) among the humanities; toward other disciplines which need the visual arts in order to realize fully their goals— anthropology, archaeology, aesthetics, history, psychology, architecture, home economics among others; toward individuals on the campus among students and faculty or in the community at large who are searching for the stability and (in a meaningful sense) recreational purpose art can bring to their personal lives; toward graduate studies in many fields; and, of course, toward students anxious to become professional artists. It is unlikely that all these obligations can be met in equal measure on every campus. Their implications cannot be avoided, however, in any college seriously interested in the teaching and practice of art.

In 1937 Arthur Pope predicted an accelerated invasion of liberal arts precincts by the artists.[7] His projection did not envisage the extent to which practitioners, once admitted, will transcend historical-theoretical limits and become—often in the manner of research scientists—searchers after new visual-structural truths. Administrators of liberal arts programs have no difficulty in justifying art history and "theory" as non-vocational (and thus respectable) materials for study. Artists, if they are added to faculties, as Pope suggested they should be, will not be contained in their influence by the teaching of theory as Pope defines it. At the risk of exerting "vocational" influence (reserved by Pope for the benefit of graduate school students) the artist must explore by doing. Theory is also historical. For better or for worse, today's artists are concerned with evocation of new insight, sometimes with necessary disregard of historical principles or accepted theory. Put another way, art theory in its large sense is conceived as being dynamic and dispersed rather than compactly unified. If the colleges cannot accept the current elements of individualism and even non-theory which characterize much of contemporary art, they should reject the artist as a practitioner on the campus, or as a serious participant in education.

7. Arthur Pope, *Art, Artist and Layman,* Cambridge: Harvard University Press, 1937.

The Museum of Art

INTRODUCTION

The college or university art museum is a relatively recent development. In the nineteenth century seven of consequence were built in the Western world: Yale (1832), Oxford (1845), Cambridge (1848), Princeton (1887), Stanford (1891), Bowdoin (1894), and Harvard (1895).

In the twentieth century, paralleling the extraordinary growth of public art museums in the United States, there has been an equally extraordinary growth of university art museums in this country.[1] While over one hundred of the institutions answering this study's questionnaire claim to have exhibition space of some kind on the campus, only some twenty can truly claim to have a building designed to provide more or less complete museum facilities. Before 1930, art museums were opened at Mount Holyoke (1901), Michigan (1910), Oberlin (1916), Vassar (1917), Minnesota (1920), Mills and Smith (1925), Williams (1926), and new and expanded buildings were acquired by Harvard (1927) and Yale (1928). During the Depression years of the 1930s and the war years of the 1940s there was an understandable lull in building, although in 1937 Williams did make a further renovation of its former library for exhibition and art teaching purposes and in 1949 Amherst opened a new art museum. In the 1950s and '60s, in quick succession, one after another college or university has built an art museum, or has one in the planning stage: California, Los Angeles (1951), Notre Dame (1952), a modern building added

1. Very few university museums were built abroad in this century and these were mainly in England: e.g. Courtauld Institute, London; Barber Institute, Birmingham; and Whitworth Art Gallery, Manchester.

at Yale (1953), Arizona (1955), North Carolina and Wellesley (1958), Pomona, Washington (St. Louis), Brandeis, Illinois (1961), Indiana, Ohio State, Nebraska, and Texas (1963). In the immediate future, Princeton, Wisconsin, Iowa, and Berkeley will open new buildings and Kansas, Minnesota, and Williams have building plans under consideration.

In addition, in the present century a number of colleges and universities have, like Williams, established art museums in buildings not designed for museum use (Michigan and Kansas, for example) and some have separately housed specialized collections such as Harvard's Germanic Museum in Cambridge, her Byzantine Institute at Dumbarton Oaks, and Chicago's Oriental Institute; or natural history museums with considerable collections of non-Western art (Harvard, Yale, Berkeley), or a collection such as that at the University of Pennsylvania which combines archaeological artifacts with works of art of the highest quality.[2]

From an examination of this tremendous growth of art museums on the campus it is clear that it has gone hand in hand with the extraordinary expansion of the teaching of the history and the practice of art in American colleges and universities. Previous chapters have dealt with history of art and studio practice at the undergraduate and graduate levels. Here we are concerned with the relationship of these two branches of art teaching to the art museum, and also the latter's relationship to the college or university as a whole.

2. A further development has been the building of art centers such as those at Dartmouth and Trinity College, Connecticut, where the visual arts and the performing arts are housed in one complex; or, as at M.I.T., where exhibition space has been provided for loan exhibitions but no provision has been made for displaying a permanent collection, nor is one contemplated.

THE MUSEUM AND ART HISTORY

Acquisitions. If the list of museums above is examined one notes to begin with that, with the exception of Harvard (always a law unto itself), nearly all of them are on campuses at some distance from a major public museum. As American art history flourished, particularly at the graduate level, and with Europe and the Orient, despite jet travel, far removed in time and distance from the classroom, the need soon became evident for the study of original works of art to mitigate, in part at least, the critical anemia that results from overexposure to mere books and photographs. Furthermore, in recent years, as one can see again from the list, the further an art department found itself from the great concentrations of original works of art in such metropolitan centers as New York, Chicago, Boston, Washington, Philadelphia, the greater became the incentive to build an art museum in close association with it.

Only a few university art museums, however, have collections of sufficient range and quality to provide a diet rich enough for even the average needs of art history students and faculty. Long established museums such as Harvard's, Yale's, and Princeton's have collections of considerable importance in more than one period of the history of art. Other museums, such as Oberlin, Smith, and Nebraska, have outstanding, though smaller, collections. Most college and university museums, however, and particularly those recently built, have as yet very modest permanent collections and must perforce depend upon frequent loan exhibitions to fill their walls. Which brings us to the major problem of such museums: acquisitions.

In the course of the present study eighteen university and college museums were visited.[3] Almost all of them complained of meager acquisition funds and of how much their museum was forced to depend upon gifts for the growth of its collection.[4] Where the alumni of a university have many discriminating collectors whose interest in the museum can be aroused, acquisitions may grow steadily in number and quality. But where alumni collectors are few, non-existent, or (perhaps worse) undiscriminating, the future of the museum with insufficient purchase funds is bleak indeed. The situation now is that in all too many instances, in our opinion, directors or curators are purchasing or accepting as gifts works of inferior quality, presumably out of sheer necessity. The correctives for the impoverished collection are three: (1) more acquisition funds; (2) an absolute insistence upon exhibiting only works of quality, however few, and resisting to the best of one's ability all offers of inferior gifts, except for sale or exchange; and (3) with limited means, resisting the temptation to buy poor works by big names or studio leavings of fashionable artists. Of course, it must be admitted that in this period of high prices, owing to a combination of economic inflation and a shrinking market in works of good quality, no matter

3. Arizona, U.C.L.A., Georgia, Harvard, Illinois, Indiana, Kansas, Michigan, Minnesota, Nebraska, North Carolina, Oberlin, Princeton, Smith, Texas, Vassar, Williams, Yale.

4. In a sample response from twenty-three institutions, including the eighteen visited, three said they were totally dependent on gifts for acquisitions; seven said 90% or more; nine said 50–90%; and only three said that purchases exceeded gifts. The acquisition budgets, 1961–62, for fourteen institutions totaled $373,000, with a high of $95,000 and a low of $1,000. Six of the fourteen said the university provided no acquisition funds. Twelve stated that the support for acquisitions came largely from alumni. Seven (all state universities) said they were not so restricted.

how much purchase funds one may have it is becoming increasingly difficult to buy anything at all of exceptional importance.[5] Certainly in the old master field it has become something of an international event when an important Rembrandt changes hands. For the museum of limited means, then—and this includes all university galleries—one alternative is to buy drawings or prints, although examples by old masters are becoming scarce and relatively expensive. Sculpture, which is somewhat less in demand by private collectors, is another possibility. Furthermore, good sculpture old and new, large and small, can still be found at prices which still seem modest when compared with those asked for most old or new paintings. In any case, the new museum would seem to be wise to specialize in one or a few areas rather than to extend its resources thinly over the whole history of art in a futile attempt to be "representative." Better one outstanding example of a period than many mediocre or fragmentary "study pieces." The fact remains, however (and this cannot be emphasized too strongly), that most academic museums, and particularly the recent ones, are in great need of additional purchase funds and these must

5. Acquisition policies at the eighteen museums studied vary considerably. Three stress the importance of acquiring objects of quality, regardless of period or kind. Three seek to build on strength. One will buy works regardless of quality if they are useful for student research. Two believe in acquiring one major object each year and a number of lesser importance. Two avoid the decorative arts. Two with limited resources concentrate on acquiring prints and drawings. Two buy against the market, avoiding the fashionable, and therefore expensive, objects. Some take neighboring public museums into account and try to avoid competition in fields of collecting. As for who authorizes purchases or the acceptance of gifts, policy varies from museum to museum. Some place full responsibility on the director. Some have acquisition committees drawn from the faculty or alumni collectors.

soon be forthcoming from public or private sources if the
new museums are to be anything more than expensive
architectural ornaments.[6]

Exhibitions. While a new museum is slowly assembling
a permanent collection it is forced to depend meanwhile
on loans to keep any sort of exhibition program going.
This is particularly true of most academic museums, as
our study has shown. Many of these exhibitions, one
finds, are prefabricated by one or other of the national
loan services and sent on tour for two or more years.
Because of the consequent length of the loan period the
quality of loans has tended more and more to suffer.
Lenders are loath to lend their best things for more than
a few months. The result is that a number of college and
university museums have found it advisable to prepare
their own exhibitions, tailoring them to particular course
needs, either in the studio or history of art departments
or addressed to the university community as a whole.
On occasion, these exhibitions are shared with another
college or university.[7] The three exhibitions of eigh-
teenth-, nineteenth-, and twentieth-century drawings prepared recently by the University of Minnesota art museum
and shared with Harvard and the Guggenheim Museum
are outstanding examples of their kind. Each has been
selected with great discrimination and well catalogued.
Another exhibition of this type, *Color in Prints,* was prepared in 1962 by a group of graduate students at Yale
under the direction of the curator of drawings and prints.
The exhibition itself was the first to explore the develop-

6. See table 12, Art Museums, *number of objects in collections.*
7. Admittedly the museum with a small staff, a limited collection,
and a limited art faculty is faced with a dilemma: however much it
may want to originate exhibitions of its own, it is forced for lack of
man-power and other resources to depend on packaged shows.

ment of the rise of color in prints from the sixteenth century to the present. It gave graduate students excellent training in the preparation of an exhibition and a scholarly catalogue and the result under wise direction was, however didactic, a beautiful selection of the finest prints available. Smith and Bowdoin have also presented medium-sized exhibitions of high quality, such as the former's show of Renaissance small bronzes and the latter's retrospective of prints by Leonard Baskin, both accompanied by superbly designed catalogues.[8]

In recent years a few public museums have turned to art history scholars from the universities for the preparation of specialized exhibitions. The Museum of Modern Art in New York has over the years asked a number of university-centered specialists to serve it in this way. Recently Harvard's Seymour Slive selected and wrote the catalogue for Haarlem's great Hals retrospective, and Yale's Robert Herbert prepared the Barbizon exhibition for the Boston Museum of Fine Arts in collaboration with the Toledo Museum of Art and the California Palace of the Legion of Honor.

Despite these examples of cooperation between the campus and the public museum such associations are all too infrequent. This seems to be particularly true when one looks at the relationship, or lack of it, between many university museums and neighboring public museums. It may be that rivalry in collecting or for the favor of

8. A word of caution here. Good, scholarly exhibitions take time to prepare. They cannot be done in the midst of a heavy loan exhibition schedule. Better fewer exhibitions, well prepared, for longer exhibition periods than a program of many shows that gives a false impression of activity and gains only ephemeral notices in the local press. Furthermore, the fewer the number of changing exhibitions, the greater the attention that can be paid to the presentation and cataloguing of permanent collections.

local patrons has too often produced a coolness between such museums, or a suspicion held often on the part of the older public museum that the college or university museum is an upstart and a potentially dangerous competitor. Where this situation exists it must be corrected if both the public and university museums are to fulfill their duties to their respective communities.

Surely an alliance of effort would be advantageous to each institution; acquisition policies can be devised that are not unnecessarily overlapping, curatorial advice can be exchanged, dual staff appointments may be found beneficial, library and lecture resources shared and, above all, collections of works of art used in common. Where the public museum over a long period has acquired a rich collection in a particular field, a collection which the university museum can never hope, nor should it attempt, to compete with, long-term loans of part of the public collection should be made available to the university museum: for longer and more precise study by faculty and students than the public visitor can be expected to give to particular works; to provide the public museum, whose curatorial staff is often limited, with scholarly research for catalogue purposes; and to bring the student into an intimate contact with original works, a contact which can never be replaced by only an occasional visit to a local public museum, particularly as with many universities in the middle and far West where the public museum may be as much as fifty or a hundred miles away.[9] In short, everyone stands to gain by collaboration. Standards of curatorial scholarship can be improved in the cataloguing and publication of public mu-

9. The further removed the university is from a major public museum, of course, the greater the incentive for the university to build a museum of its own.

seum collections by closer collaboration with university scholars, and the scholarship of the faculty can be enlivened and improved by close, day to day examination of original works of art.

Curators and scholarship. For all this exchange of ideas and energies to happen, to repeat, there must be a removal of suspicion between museum curators and university scholars. The curator is too often prone to sneer at the university man's preoccupation with abstract scholarship, derived from a study of books and photographs; the university scholar, on his part, looks upon many curators as superficial showmen and second-class scholars, unable or unwilling to do serious research. In too many instances both parties are guilty to some degree of the accusations leveled against them; but in our study we have found encouraging signs, few though they may be at present, that the problems of collaboration are being recognized. In particular, the source of the trouble has to be faced at the graduate level of art history teaching. The prospective curator has for too long been selected from the less scholarly lower half of a class, a student with some "flair" for the subject but unable or unwilling to devote himself for enough years to the strenuous requirements of the most advanced graduate degree, the Ph.D. Such a student has been permitted to leave with an M.A. degree and thereafter has been held in a certain contempt by his Ph.D. colleagues and he in turn, probably from some sense of insecurity derived from a lower academic degree, has charged his teacher colleagues with unimaginative pseudo-scientific pedantry. It must be recognized now that the period of massive acquisitions by museums is over, a period when the personable though only partially trained curators struggled, often with pleasure and excitement, to care for the flood of gifts and purchases that has come to American museums over the past fifty years. Consolidation and selective weeding of good works from bad and the correction of many overly optimistic attributions is now in order. To achieve this result, the scholarship of both the teaching and curatorial fraternities must be placed on an equal level and the preparation for this scholarship must also be on a single standard of high performance.[10] To put it briefly, connoisseurship, "flair," a "good eye," without the ability to control enthusiasms by precise research, is dangerous; precise research without an eye for the relative quality of the object or objects being studied can lead to a sterile, bookish art history.

All easier said than done. The administrative pattern of our largely privately financed public museums must change to attract young scholars to the museum field. Trustee and directorial responsibilities must be more clearly defined and separated, the former to restrict themselves to overall policy and financial questions, the latter to the maintenance of professional standards of acquisition, scholarship, display, and publication. Curatorial staffs must be given more time with pay away from their day to day duties in the museum to do serious research, and salaries must be placed on a more equitable basis, commensurate with corresponding faculty positions in the university. Parallels in rank and compensation should

10. To this end a museum training program has recently been instituted at Yale, financed by the Ford Foundation, which provides a number of pre-doctoral and post-doctoral fellowships requiring a part- or full-time year's residence in the University Art Gallery with the possible extension of the fellowship for a second year. Ford Foundation grants for curatorial training have also been made to the Institute of Fine Arts, New York University, and to five public art museums in Cleveland, Toledo, Minneapolis, Kansas City, Mo., and Worcester, Mass.

be established between museum personnel and university teachers, e.g. a curator or associate curator should equal a professor or associate professor, an assistant curator should be on a level with an assistant professor, and so on down the line. The university museum is in a position to lead the way in establishing such parallel appointments and by its example it eventually may influence public museums to do likewise.[11] One word of caution: parallel *titles* are not enough; salaries and perquisites, particularly vacations, pension provisions, and tenure at the rank of curator, must also be on a reasonably equal basis.

THE MUSEUM AND THE STUDIO PROGRAM

The interviews conducted by this study indicate that the average studio teacher is much less interested in the art museum as a teaching instrument than his art history colleague.[12] The reasons for this are not far to seek. In the present post-academic phase of art practice, study of older works for technical purposes has fallen into some

11. At present, appointment practice varies widely in the university museums visited. At one institution the director is the equivalent of a dean and is on a five-year appointment. At another he has an academic appointment as professor but is on a five-year appointment as director. At six he is appointed as a professor, with tenure. At two he is also chairman of the art department and in this capacity thinks of himself as superior to himself as director. At three the director is the equivalent of an associate professor (two by academic appointment, one as an assimilated rank). For curators and assistant curators there is an equally wide range of title equivalents. Some curators have the rank of professor, by academic appointment. Others have the equivalent rank of anything from instructor to associate professor. Assistant curators are more commonly associated with the title and perquisites of an instructor, but serve the museum on an eleven- rather than a nine-month basis.

12. Of the eighteen museums visited, only two schools considered that the museum's highest responsibility was to the studio program.

disrepute.[13] Copying of old masters, for example, is not
encouraged by studio teachers, although in one school
we did find a revival of this ancient practice. Present
studio requirements, on the other hand, seem to demand
a program of changing exhibitions of contemporary art,
either produced by the faculty or students themselves, or
representing some aspect of art of current interest. No
implied criticism of studio teachers' particular requirements of the art museum is intended here. Since their
approach to art history is necessarily unsystematic and
biased in favor of art that has a special relation to their
own creative drives, a "comprehensive" museum collection is of less interest to such artist-teachers and their stu-

13. One art school dean has written to us as follows:

   The museum as a force in teaching studio subjects appears to
   have declined significantly in almost all schools, campus-based
   or independent, since the war. Responsibility for the introduction
   of young artists to the museum as an enlightening force is in-
   cumbent on a group of artist-teachers whose own convictions
   have been developed by (among other things, of course) the
   museum experience. A "walk-through" with a class is hardly
   more significant to art students than the docent-led excursions
   to the museum are for grade schoolers—at least they are not
   more significant if there is no completion of problems which
   contain a museum factor. The enthusiasms with which new
   movements in art are embraced and the speed at which they
   are used up in the colleges is an indication of a speedup in studio
   education which bypasses historical record in favor of current
   values. The significance of art historical record as a force in
   developing really new attitudes and in the recognition of qualities
   and quality in art is diminishing. Artists who are teaching are
   trapped by the *ab initio* syndrome, which really is an abdication
   of their powers of influence and leadership. They can see (perhaps because of their own careful scrutiny of the past) the way
   the present moves young students to increasing confidence in the
   infallibility of their own judgments. It appears to me that in this
   confusion of purposes, art comes off badly, and students emerge
   from this truncated educational experience as people who are
   literate only in their own terms.

dents than individual works of the past and present that feed their own needs for formal and coloristic experiment. Actually, this specialized approach to art, this intensely selfish, if you like, consumption of art, can be a very valuable corrective to a collecting policy of acquiring objects of more historical than artistic importance. The artist's eye may see through the technical or emotional shortcomings of a work of art more quickly than a curator whose judgment of artistic values may have become clouded by historical or iconographic considerations.

With reference to the artist-teacher and the museum, one important phenomenon has been demonstrated by this study on a statistical basis: the farther west the college or university is in the United States, the larger the studio program is likely to be and the smaller the number of art historians on the same faculty. This factor has a significant bearing on the art museum on the campus. With small or non-existent permanent collections, the art historian is given little or no food for his researches, aside from changing loan exhibitions. The studio use of the museum, where a studio faculty is dominant, is likely to emphasize exhibitions of contemporary art for its own purposes. And by not emphasizing permanent acquisitions the studio faculty may consciously or unconsciously retard the development of a museum in a conventional or comprehensive direction, holding it to the status of an "art center" rather than an art museum. For many reasons previously stated, the new middle and far western university museums can hardly expect for some time to come to be anything more than buildings devoted in the main to changing loan shows. It is to be hoped, however, that as a better balance is established between art history and studio faculties a greater emphasis will be placed on the long-term viewing of individual works of art, both by long-term loans from neighboring public museums and by permanent acquisition.

THE MUSEUM AND DEPARTMENTS OTHER THAN ART

Ideally, a university museum should serve as far as possible the whole university, not just the art historian or studio teacher.[14] No doubt the needs of the art faculty must be the museum's first consideration, but not to the exclusion of departments of literature, history, language, and even science. The weaker the museum collection is, of course, the less use can be made of it by any one department. But by a carefully planned program of exhibitions and lectures, departments other than art can and should be attracted to the museum and there find a meeting ground with their art colleagues. This study has revealed few examples of the art museum, however good its intentions, serving as more than a very informal bridge between the various divisions of the humanities.[15] Lack of communication between these divisions is all too common at present, as everyone knows, and the art faculty is not wholly to blame for a condition characteristic of the faculty as a whole. However, the art historian in particular, because of the diverse range of his interests, extending as they do to languages, literature, history, sociology, psychology, and so forth, is in a peculiarly advantageous position to encourage a greater rapport between the hu-

14. Thirteen of the eighteen museums felt their greatest responsibility was to the academic community as a whole.

15. Five institutions reported no use of the museum by departments other than art. Thirteen said there was *some* use by departments of English and history (six each), area studies (five), languages (five), philosophy (one), classics (one), anthropology (one), and drama (one).

manistic disciplines. The art museum may well be one of his principal instruments in achieving this community of outlook.[16]

THE BUILDING

So far we have dealt with the role of the art museum on the campus. What of the building itself and its staff? First, the building. Of the eighteen museums examined in detail during the course of this study, no one can be considered a model of excellence in every respect. Some are wasteful of space or spatially inadequate. Some are indifferently lighted; others show a thoughtful fusion of daylight and artificial light. Most suffer from frightening staff deficiencies. Sites and resources differ widely and therefore no one building or administrative formula is suitable or possible in all instances.[17] But certain minimum requirements can be outlined on the basis of our experience throughout this study, and where one or another museum finds itself operating below the minimum standards here proposed, our recommendations may have some value in helping it to correct existing deficiencies

16. In this connection, where the collections of a university museum are sufficiently advanced a scholarly, profusely illustrated catalogue, prepared by faculty curators assisted by graduate students, is an absolute necessity, not only for the art department itself but for the use of all other university departments. Regrettably, in 1961–62 this study found that only one of the eighteen museums visited had a comprehensive catalogue publication program underway.

17. Of the eighteen museums visited twelve are housed in buildings specially built for museum use. Six are not. Fourteen share their building with other departments. However, thirteen share with a related department (history of art, studio, etc.). Only one said their building was completely adequate. Eight said adequate, but not for the future. Nine said inadequate, four of them being in buildings not designed as museums. Three plan new buildings and two have new buildings going up.

where this has not been made impossible by an architectural straitjacket.

First, where the site permits, the building should be no more than two stories high, with a deep basement for storage and other maintenance facilities. Passenger elevators should be avoided where possible, since they have proved to be a continuous traffic bottleneck at periods of peak attendance. A freight elevator is, however, absolutely necessary for the safe transport of works of art from floor to floor, and can on occasion be used by the occasional visitor suffering from a disability which precludes his using a staircase.

Exhibition and storage space should be commodious and, above all, *flexible*.[18] A large room that can be divided up easily by temporary panels is preferable to a series of smaller rooms whose spaces are fixed. The ratio of exhibition to storage and maintenance space for a university gallery should be on the order of fifty-fifty, with some of this storage and maintenance space adjoining exhibition rooms and some in the basement. Adjoining storage space is a necessary convenience to permit installations of changing exhibitions and to provide easy access by advanced students to material in storage, for individual study or seminar purposes. Basement storage should be used mainly for works not in frequent use or for the temporary storage of a large part of the permanent collection when display rooms are needed for a major loan exhibition.

Lighting should never be wholly artificial and for works of art, particularly paintings, never fluorescent. (To date no fluorescent lamp known to us does not dis-

---

18. See table 13, *Percentage of gallery space devoted to various functions.*

tort color values to some degree.) Daylight at its best will always be ideal for works of art. Supplementary artificial light should be incandescent, with spots or flood lamps, and arranged on as flexible a system as possible to provide for numerous location changes of paintings and sculpture. While daylight is best for works of art, one can have too much of it if it is at the expense of hanging space for the works of art themselves. Glass walls are useless for hanging paintings. Daylight from a north wall or from overhead is preferable to all other directions, as artists have known for centuries.

The shipping room and carpenter shop should adjoin the loading platform. The registrar's office and examining room should be directly connected with the shipping room. The conservator's and photographer's studios should be as near as possible to the registrar and the shipping room. Wood floors are preferable to stone, cement, tile, or carpet. They are long lasting, easy to keep clean and relatively resilient—a factor in helping to control the incidence of "museum feet." There should be facilities for the control of temperature and humidity throughout the building.

THE STAFF

We turn now to minimum staff requirements.[19] If the museum is of any considerable size a full-time director is an absolute necessity. Too many university museums are attempting part-time direction by a department chairman or some other faculty member.[20] Even where a collection

---

19. See table 14, *Art museum staff*.

20. Of eighteen museums visited, directors of nine give full time to position, one gives three-quarters time, four half-time, and four one-third time.

is small, the preparation and installation of loan exhibitions is a full-time job, together with the active exploration of an acquisitions program. It is false economy or a misguided refusal to delegate authority that is responsible for a part-time directorship policy. Its consequences are felt throughout the museum—in the performance of the rest of the staff, the quality of exhibitions offered, and the maintenance of the building.

Other minimum staff requirements are a full-time secretary to the director, preferably one with some bookkeeping experience; a registrar, full- or part-time, depending upon the size of the collection and the frequency of changing exhibitions; a full- or part-time photographer; a resident or visiting conservator, again depending on the size of the collection; and a full-time building superintendent who is proficient in packing, unpacking, hanging and installing works of art under curatorial direction, and who will supervise the cleaning and maintenance of the building. Where the collection is large the museum will also need an experienced carpenter, preferably a cabinetmaker, who can prepare shipping crates and make sculpture pedestals and display cases. The smaller museum may have to be content with a superintendent who is a professional carpenter. Finally, a guard force should be large enough to give adequate protection for all exhibition rooms. Our study has shown that one of the greatest staff deficiencies in university museums is lack of guards. In a few instances the force consists of one man or a scholarship student whose unhappy responsibility is the protection of all the exhibition rooms of the museum. The consequences of an inadequate guard force or maintenance staff are obviously serious. Thefts may result, works of art may be damaged by inexperienced handling and packing, insurance rates are likely to in-

crease, and other museums or private collectors may re-
fuse to lend objects of any real value.

CONSERVATION

All museums have as a primary responsibility the care
and conservation of the works of art in their charge. The
number of professional conservators in America is totally
inadequate for the proper conservation of our large public and our many private collections. The training of conservators is a slow process and all too few are being
trained at present. Most museums provide far too little
in their budgets for conservation. As with animal bodies
or machines, if the deterioration of a work of art is allowed to pass beyond a certain point, a condition of
health is hard to recover. Admittedly, many small museums cannot afford a resident conservator and even if
they can a good man is hard to find. The best alternative
seems to have been found by several museums banding
together and sharing a conservator on a visiting, periodic
check basis. A good example is the Intermuseum Conservation Association, which serves eleven museums and
has its headquarters at Oberlin.

CONCLUSION

At the risk of ending on an unduly pessimistic note, it
must be admitted that however phenomenal the growth
of university art museums has been in this country over
the past few decades, most of them are still in an embry-
onic state. Their permanent collections are small or non-
existent and, in competition with rich private buyers or
well-endowed public museums, they are likely to remain
so for many years to come. It behooves most art depart-

ments, therefore, not to assume that, though the permanent collection of their museum may be small, in time it will be enlarged; and that, meanwhile, loan exhibitions are sufficient for most teaching needs. This is a dangerous illusion. Nothing can take the place for the foreseeable future of the large comprehensive public collections in our major cities and abroad. Consequently, if he is to achieve maturity the would-be art historian or artist must travel great distances and must expose himself for long periods of time to the works of art of the past and present. It is these works, after all, when absorbed in all their fabulous diversity, that feed the imaginations of the artist and the scholar, each according to his needs.

Appendices

LIST OF INSTITUTIONS STUDIED

The thirty institutions in italics were those selected for particular study.

University of Arizona, Tucson, Arizona
Brown University, Providence, Rhode Island
Bryn Mawr College, Bryn Mawr, Pennsylvania
University of California at Berkeley, California
University of California at Los Angeles, California
Carnegie Institute of Technology, Pittsburgh, Pennsylvania
University of Chicago, Chicago, Illinois
Columbia University, New York, New York
University of Georgia, Athens, Georgia
Harvard University, Cambridge, Massachusetts
University of Illinois, Urbana, Illinois
Indiana University, Bloomington, Indiana
State University of Iowa, Iowa City, Iowa
University of Kansas, Lawrence, Kansas
University of Michigan, Ann Arbor, Michigan
University of Minnesota, Minneapolis, Minnesota
University of Nebraska, Lincoln and Omaha, Nebraska
New York University, New York, New York
University of North Carolina, Chapel Hill, North Carolina
Oberlin College, Oberlin, Ohio
Ohio State University, Columbus, Ohio
University of Pennsylvania, Philadelphia, Pennsylvania
Princeton University, Princeton, New Jersey
Smith College, Northampton, Massachusetts
University of Texas, Austin, Texas
Vassar College, Poughkeepsie, New York
Washington University, St. Louis, Missouri

Williams College, Williamstown, Massachusetts
University of Wisconsin, Madison, Wisconsin
Yale University, New Haven, Connecticut
Adelphi University, Garden City, New York
Agnes Scott College, Decatur, Georgia
Alabama College, Montevallo, Alabama
University of Alabama, University, Alabama
University of Alaska, College, Alaska
Albion College, Albion, Michigan
Alverno College, Milwaukee, Wisconsin
American University, Washington, D.C.
Amherst College, Amherst, Massachusetts
Andrews University, Berrien Springs, Michigan
Anna Maria College, Paxton, Massachusetts
Arizona State College, Flagstaff, Arizona
University of Arkansas, Fayetteville, Arkansas
Duke University, Durham, North Carolina
Dunbarton College of Holy Cross, Washington, D.C.
Earlham College, Richmond, Indiana
East Carolina College, Greenville, North Carolina
East Central State College, Ada, Oklahoma
Eastern Illinois University, Charleston, Illinois
Eastern Michigan University, Ypsilanti, Michigan
East Tennessee State College, Johnson City, Tennessee
Emory University, Atlanta, Georgia
Findlay College, Findlay, Ohio
Flint Junior College, Flint, Michigan
Florida Presbyterian College, St. Petersburg, Florida
Florida State University, Tallahassee, Florida
University of Florida, Gainesville, Florida
Furman University, Greenville, South Carolina
Georgia State College, Atlanta, Georgia
Georgian Court College, Lakewood, New Jersey
Goucher College, Towson, Maryland

Grambling College, Grambling, Louisiana
Grove City College, Grove City, Pennsylvania
Harpur College, Binghamton, New York
University of Hawaii, Honolulu, Hawaii
Hollins College, Roanoke, Virginia
Holy Apostles Seminary, Cromwell, Connecticut
Holy Family College, Torresdale, Philadelphia, Pennsylvania
Hope College, Holland, Michigan
University of Houston, Houston, Texas
Illinois Wesleyan University, Bloomington, Illinois
Iowa State University, Iowa City, Iowa
Jacksonville University, Jacksonville, Florida
Jersey City State College, Jersey City, New Jersey
Johns Hopkins University, Baltimore, Maryland
Kalamazoo College, Kalamazoo, Michigan
Kansas State College, Manhattan, Kansas
Kansas Wesleyan University, Salina, Kansas
Kearney State College, Kearney, Nebraska
Kent State University, Kent, Ohio
Kenyon College, Gambier, Ohio
Lafayette College, Easton, Pennsylvania
Lehigh University, Bethlehem, Pennsylvania
Lincoln University, Lincoln University, Pennsylvania
Linfield College, McMinnville, Oregon
Longwood College, Farmville, Virginia
Louisiana Polytechnic Institute, Ruston, Louisiana
Louisiana State University, Baton Rouge, Louisiana
University of Louisville, Louisville, Kentucky
Lycoming College, Williamsport, Pennsylvania
McNeese State College, Lake Charles, Louisiana
Madonna College, Livonia, Michigan
Manhattanville College of the Sacred Heart, Purchase, New York

Marian College, Indianapolis, Indiana
Mary Baldwin College, Staunton, Virginia
Marymount College, Palos Verdes Estates, California
Marywood College, Scranton, Pennsylvania
Massachusetts College of Art, Boston, Massachusetts
University of Massachusetts, Amherst, Massachusetts
Memphis State University, Memphis, Tennessee
Meredith College, Raleigh, North Carolina
Meridian Municipal Junior College, Meridian, Mississippi
Merrimack College, Andover, Massachusetts
University of Miami, Coral Gables, Florida
Miami University, Oxford, Ohio
Michigan State University, East Lansing, Michigan
Middle Tennessee State College, Murfreesboro,
   Tennessee
Midland College, Fremont, Nebraska
Midwestern University, Wichita Falls, Texas
Millersville State College, Millersville, Pennsylvania
Mills College, Oakland, California
Milwaukee-Downer College, Milwaukee, Wisconsin
Minot State College, Minot, North Dakota
Mississippi College, Clinton, Mississippi
University of Missouri at Kansas City, Missouri
Monmouth College, Monmouth, Illinois
Montana State University, Missoula, Montana
Montclair State College, Upper Montclair, New Jersey
Mount Holyoke College, South Hadley, Massachusetts
Mount Mary College, Milwaukee, Wisconsin
Mount San Antonio College, Walnut, California
Mount Union College, Alliance, Ohio
Mundelein College, Chicago, Illinois
Museum School of Art, Houston, Texas
Nazareth College, Nazareth, Michigan
University of Nevada, Reno, Nevada

New Bedford Institute of Technology, New Bedford,
    Massachusetts
University of New Hampshire, Durham, New Hampshire
New Mexico Highlands University, Las Vegas, New
    Mexico
New Mexico State University, University Park, New
    Mexico
University of New Mexico, Albuquerque, New Mexico
North Carolina College at Durham, North Carolina
Northeastern University, Boston, Massachusetts
Northern Illinois University, DeKalb, Illinois
Northwest Nazarene College, Nampa, Idaho
Northwestern University, Evanston, Illinois
University of Notre Dame, Notre Dame, Indiana
Oakland City College, Oakland City, Indiana
Occidental College, Los Angeles, California
Ohio University, Athens, Ohio
University of Oklahoma, Norman, Oklahoma
Orange County Community Junior College, Middle-
    town, New York
Oregon State University, Corvallis, Oregon
Our Lady of Cincinnati College, Cincinnati, Ohio
Our Lady of the Lake College, San Antonio, Texas
Pepperdine College, Los Angeles, California
Pomona College, Claremont, California
Purdue University, Lafayette, Indiana
Queens College, Flushing, New York
Quincy College, Quincy, Illinois
Randolph-Macon Woman's College, Lynchburg,
    Virginia
Regis College, Weston, Massachusetts
Rensselaer Polytechnic Institute, Troy, New York
Rice University, Houston, Texas
University of Rochester, Rochester, New York

Rockford College, Rockford, Illinois
Rollins College, Winterpark, Florida
Rosary Hill College, Buffalo, New York
Rutgers University, New Brunswick, New Jersey
Sacramento State College, Sacramento, California
Salem College, Winston-Salem, North Carolina
Sarah Lawrence College, Bronxville, New York
College of Saint Catherine, St. Paul, Minnesota
College of St. Francis, Joliet, Illinois
St. John's University, Collegeville, Minnesota
St. John's University, Jamaica, New York
St. Joseph's College for Women, Brooklyn, New York
St. Lawrence University, Canton, New York
St. Louis University, St. Louis, Missouri
Saint Mary's College, Notre Dame, Indiana
Shorter College, Rome, Georgia
Skidmore College, Saratoga Springs, New York
University of South Carolina, Columbia, South Carolina
University of South Florida, Tampa, Florida
Southern Connecticut State College, New Haven,
    Connecticut
Southern State Teachers College, Springfield, South
    Dakota
Spring Hill College, Mobile, Alabama
Stanford University, Stanford, California
State University of New York College of Ceramics at
    Alfred University, Alfred, New York
State University College at Buffalo, Buffalo, New York
State University College at Oswego, Oswego, New York
State University College at Potsdam, Potsdam, New York
Swarthmore College, Swarthmore, Pennsylvania
Sweet Briar College, Sweet Briar, Virginia
University of Tennessee, Knoxville, Tennessee
Texas College of Art and Industries, Kingsville, Texas

Toledo Museum of Art School of Design, Toledo, Ohio
Trenton Junior College, Trenton, New Jersey
Tufts College, Medford, Massachusetts
Tulane University, New Orleans, Louisiana
Union College, Schenectady, New York
University of Utah, Salt Lake City, Utah
Valparaiso University, Valparaiso, Indiana
Villa Madonna College, Covington, Kentucky
University of Virginia, Charlottesville, Virginia
Wabash College, Crawfordsville, Indiana
Washington State University, Pullman, Washington
University of Washington, Seattle, Washington
Wayne State University, Detroit, Michigan
Wellesley College, Wellesley, Massachusetts
Wesleyan College, Macon, Georgia
Wesleyan University, Middletown, Connecticut
West Liberty State College, West Liberty, West Virginia
West Virginia University, Morgantown, West Virginia
Western Illinois University, Macomb, Illinois
Western Washington State College, Bellingham,
    Washington
Wheaton College, Norton, Massachusetts
Wheeling College, Wheeling, West Virginia
Willamette University, Salem, Oregon
College of William and Mary, Williamsburg, Virginia
Wilson College, Chambersburg, Pennsylvania
Wisconsin State College, Eau Claire, Wisconsin
Wisconsin State College, Stevens Point, Wisconsin
University of Wisconsin at Milwaukee, Wisconsin
Wittenberg University, Springfield, Ohio
Woman's College of Georgia, Milledgeville, Georgia
Woman's College of the University of North Carolina,
    Greensboro, North Carolina

STATISTICAL TABLES

TABLE 1   Undergraduate enrollment, all departments

Institution	1961–62	1950–51	1940–41
Arizona	12,100	5,400	2,500
Brown	3,300	3,300	1,900
Bryn Mawr	700	600	500
Berkeley	15,900	16,600	13,700
U.C.L.A.	12,700	11,100	8,200
Carnegie Institute	700	700	500
Chicago	2,200	1,900	1,600
Columbia	5,100	4,900	2,600
Georgia	7,800	5,300	3,000
Harvard	5,900	5,700	4,300
Illinois	18,300	13,500	11,100
Indiana	11,800	7,900	4,700
Iowa	9,300	6,800	5,600
Kansas	8,100	6,000	3,300
Michigan	15,700	11,600	8,300
Minnesota	26,300	18,500	13,600
Nebraska	8,000	7,000	6,100
North Carolina	6,600	5,200	3,200
Oberlin	1,700	1,500	1,300
Ohio State	21,000	14,600	10,000
Pennsylvania	5,600	6,800	5,500
Princeton	3,100	3,000	2,400
Smith	2,300	2,100	2,000
Texas	20,400	12,900	10,200
Vassar	1,500	1,400	1,200
Washington (St. Louis)	17,000	16,000	8,400
Williams	1,100	1,000	900
Wisconsin	14,700	11,600	9,500
Yale	3,900	4,300	3,100
TOTAL	262,800	207,200	140,200
High	26,300	18,500	13,700
Low	700	600	500
Average	9,060	7,140	4,830

TABLE 2   Number of students enrolled in undergraduate
          courses, autumn 1961

Institution	History of art	Studio program	Combined program
Arizona	1,619	127	
Brown			414
Bryn Mawr	86		
Berkeley			2,250
U.C.L.A.			3,913
Carnegie Institute	120	279	
Chicago	185	68	
Columbia	1,111	166	
Georgia	263	576	
Harvard	632		
Illinois	521	2,677	
Indiana	648	350	
Iowa			455
Kansas	260	525	
Michigan	1,121	488	
Minnesota	900	1,371	
Nebraska	229	694	
N.Y.U.	691	200	
North Carolina	284	156	
Ohio State	1,111	2,788	
Pennsylvania	722	28	
Princeton	476		
Smith			1,069
Texas	561	982	
Vassar	418	70	
Washington (St. Louis)	573	374	
Williams			297
Wisconsin	832	700	
Yale	1,101		
TOTAL	14,464	12,619	8,398
High	1,619	2,788	3,913
Low	86	28	297
Average	628.8	664.1	1,399.6

TABLE 3 Number of students graduating with a major in art history, studio program, or combined program

Institution	Art history			Studio program			Combined program		
	1961–62	1950–51	1940–41	1961–62	1950–51	1940–41	1961–62	1950–51	1940–41
Arizona	22	17	1	21	15	1			4
Brown	6	7	9				42	24	
Bryn Mawr									—
Berkeley							70	45	15
U.C.L.A.							146	114	
Carnegie Institute				42	35	20			
Chicago	2	1	1	6	6	—			
Columbia	42	—	—	7	6	—			
Georgia	6	—	—	32	30	10			
Harvard	66	73	24	78	58	22			
Illinois	2	0	0						
Indiana	6	2	—	30	30	1			
Iowa							28	58	30
Kansas	4	0	—	39	64	—			
Michigan	15	8	4	71	37	—			
Minnesota							37	18	—

Nebraska	20	15	7	38	62	42	29	19	17
N.Y.U.	15	—	—	21	—	—			
North Carolina	7	8	15	—					
Oberlin	4	6	—						
Ohio State	8	—	—	69	98				
Pennsylvania	10	3	5						
Princeton									
Smith	8	—	—	55	42	—	72	32	52
Texas	9	18	21						
Vassar	18	10	2						
Washington (St. Louis)				40 (BFA)	48 (BFA)	7 (Certificate)			
Williams	11	6	4						
Wisconsin	5	2	3	50	77	30			
Yale	13	—	—						
TOTAL	299	176	96	599	608	126	424	310	118
High	66	73	24	78	98	42	146	114	52
Low	2	0	0	6	6	0	28	18	4
Average	13.5	11	7.3	39.9	43.4	15.7	60.5	44.2	23.6

TABLE 4   Graduate enrollment, all departments

Institution	1961–62	1950–51	1940–41
Arizona	1,900	300	200
Bryn Mawr	300	100	200
Berkeley	7,900	5,600	3,400
U.C.L.A.	6,200	3,200	1,000
Chicago	3,700	5,000	2,800
Columbia	7,300	7,100	4,200
Georgia	900	500	300
Harvard	7,200	6,200	4,900
Illinois	4,800	3,700	1,300
Indiana	4,300	2,800	700
Iowa	2,400	2,300	1,100
Kansas	1,800	900	400
Michigan	—	7,900	3,800
Minnesota	4,500	3,600	1,400
Nebraska	1,400	1,000	400
North Carolina	1,700	1,200	700
Ohio State	4,100	2,800	1,100
Pennsylvania	2,200	900	1,100
Princeton	800	500	300
Smith	100	100	100
Texas	2,700	3,100	900
Washington (St. Louis)	900	700	300
Williams	100	—	—
Wisconsin	4,400	3,100	1,200
Yale	4,300	3,500	2,600
TOTAL	75,900	66,200	34,500
High	7,900	7,900	4,900
Average	2,810	2,450	1,270

TABLE 5   Total graduate enrollment by major, 1961–62[1]

Institution	Art history	Studio program	Combined program
Arizona	15		
Bryn Mawr	5		
Berkeley	63	42	
U.C.L.A.			180
Carnegie Institute		15	
Chicago	28	20	
Columbia	871	189	
Georgia	20	160	
Harvard	70		
Illinois	10	25	
Indiana			55
Iowa	235	625	
Kansas	6	48	
Michigan	131	36	
Minnesota	28	11	
N.Y.U.	180	137	
North Carolina	12	7	
Oberlin	13	5	
Ohio State	7	35	
Pennsylvania	240		
Princeton	23		
Texas	4	23	
Washington (St. Louis)	4		
Wisconsin	32	79	
Yale	35	160	
TOTAL	2,032	1,617	235
High	871	625	180
Low	4	5	55
Average	92.3	95.1	117.5

1. Some institutions reported total course enrollment rather than the actual number of graduate students enrolled. See p. 15 of this report.

TABLE 6   Percentage of Ph.D. students graduating within the
           five years previous to 1961–62 who became college
           or university teachers

Institution	Percentage
Bryn Mawr	99
Berkeley	90
Chicago	90
Columbia	99
Harvard	70
Iowa	99
Michigan	80
Minnesota	99
N.Y.U.	55
Ohio State	95
Pennsylvania	99
Princeton	90
Wisconsin	99
Yale	75
High	99
Low	55
Average	88.5

TABLE 7   Ranking of institutions by percentage of Ph.D. dissertations produced in various periods of time

1930–62 (453 theses)		1930–49 (123 theses)		1950–62 (330 theses)	
Harvard	28.9	Harvard	43.1	Harvard	23.6
N.Y.U. (i)	12.6	N.Y.U. (i)	11.4	N.Y.U. (i)	13.0
Princeton	10.4	N.Y.U. (e)	8.9	Princeton	10.9
Yale	7.5	Princeton	8.9	Columbia	8.8
Columbia	7.3	Yale	7.3	Yale	7.6
N.Y.U. (e)	6.2	Chicago	6.5	Iowa	6.7
Chicago	5.1	Wisconsin	4.1	N.Y.U. (e)	5.2
Iowa	4.9	Columbia	3.3	Ohio	5.2
Ohio	4.0	Bryn Mawr	2.4	Chicago	4.6
Michigan	3.8	Michigan	2.4	Michigan	4.2
Wisconsin	2.9	Ohio	.8	Berkeley	3.3
Berkeley	2.4	Washington	.8	Wisconsin	2.4
Bryn Mawr	1.6			Minnesota	1.5
Minnesota	1.1			Bryn Mawr	1.2
Johns Hopkins	.9			Johns Hopkins	1.2
Northwestern	.2			Northwestern	.3
Pennsylvania	.2			Pennsylvania	.3
Washington	.2				

(i): Institute of Fine Arts
(e): Department of Education

TABLE 8   Percentages of Ph.D. dissertations by field

	1930–39 Total: 46	*1940–49* Total: 78	*1950–59* Total: 242	*1960–62* Total: 87	*1930–62* Total: 453
Ancient	13	12	7	8	9
Medieval	35	18	16	15	18
Renaissance	24	10	12	15	14
17th and 18th centuries	2	3	11	8	8
19th century	2	9	11	15	10
20th century	7	1	3	8	4
Far East	2	5	7	3	6
Near East	2	3	1	1	1
U.S. and Canada	7	26	18	15	17
Latin America	0	0	2	2	2
Primitive, African	0	0	1	0	1
Education	4	10	3	8	5
Other	2	3	8	1	5

TABLE 9   M.F.A. degrees awarded, 1930–62

Institution	(a) Number of degrees	(b) Number of years needed to obtain degree
Carnegie Institute	28	2
Chicago	11	2
Columbia	59	2
Georgia	87	2
Illinois	107	2
Indiana	77	2
Iowa	708	3
Kansas	49	2
Michigan	67	3
Minnesota	36	3
North Carolina	10	2
Ohio State	226	2
Texas	6	2
Wisconsin	35	3
Yale	250	3
TOTAL	1,756	
High	708	3
Low	6	1
Average	117	2.2

TABLE 10 Career choices for recipients of M.F.A. degrees within the five years previous to 1961–62 (studio program)

Institution	Independent creative work	University teaching	Professional school teaching	Public-private school teaching	Museum work	Commercial work
Arizona	5%	10%		30%		30%
Brown				99%		
Berkeley	10%	15%		5%		
U.C.L.A.	15%	10%		25%	5%	45%
Carnegie Institute	40%	33.3%	26.3%			
Chicago		90%		10%		
Columbia	1%	35%	5%	57%	1%	1%
Georgia	15%	30%	10%	30%	5%	10%
Illinois		85%				15%
Indiana	30%	50%		10%		10%
Iowa	1%	90%		4%	1%	1%
Kansas	7%	40%		46%		7%
Michigan	50%	5%	2%	20%	1%	22%

Minnesota		90%	10%			
N.Y.U.	5%	40%	5%	40%	3%	3%
North Carolina	4%	30%		40%	4%	22%
Oberlin	5%	40%	10%	5%	5%	
Ohio	4%	91%		5%		
Texas	16%	68%	16%			
Wisconsin	2%	25%	4%	50%	2%	12%
Yale	7%	60%	7%	7%		25%
High	50%	91%	16%	99%	5%	45%
Low	1%	5%	2%	4%	1%	1%
Average	11%	49.7%	7.6%	28.4%	3%	15.6%

TABLE 11 Total scholarship aid given by institution or
department, 1961–62, in dollars

| | *Studio program* | | *Art history* | |
Institution	Under-graduate	Graduate	Under-graduate	Graduate
Arizona	1,500			
Bryn Mawr			4,800	6,300
Berkeley		2,000		3,600
U.C.L.A.	800	5,000	800	6,500
Carnegie Institute	32,400	2,800		
Columbia		16,000		40,100
Georgia	1,100	4,300	700	3,200
Harvard				55,200
Indiana				2,000
Iowa	300	2,000	300	700
Michigan	4,000			13,600
Minnesota	500			1,000
Nebraska	300			
N.Y.U.	12,500	6,000		43,000
Oberlin		1,800		5,400
Pennsylvania				2,000
Princeton				55,000
Texas	1,900	200		
Vassar	500			
Washington (St. Louis)	20,500			
Williams	2,000		5,000	
Wisconsin		11,700		4,500
Yale		35,000		32,000
TOTAL	78,300	86,800	11,600	274,100
High	32,400	35,000	5,000	55,200
Low		200	300	700
Average	5,590	7,890	2,320	17,130

TABLE 12 Art museum, Number of objects in collections (estimates in some instances), 1961–62

Institution	Ancient	Near Eastern	Far Eastern	Medieval	Renaissance and Baroque	18th–19th century	20th century	Drawings	Prints	Decorative arts	Other (Pre-Columbian, African, etc.)
Arizona	20		125		67	25	255	20	50		
Berkeley			85			400	30		200		
U.C.L.A.	20	20	25		60	35	100	1,000	9,000	25	75
Columbia	200		200		3	40	60				
Georgia			300		12	16	500	22	450		
Harvard	880	511	4,500	275	820	1,355	980	3,500	42,891	1,530	910
Illinois		1	452	2	28	37	232	51	380	132	
Indiana	200	50	100	30	25	20	50	50	100	50	200
Iowa			2		2	3	125	20	135	14	40
Kansas	103	12	2,730	70	168	164	80	60	600	1,650	10
Michigan		100	500	20	30	225	150	575	2,200		
Minnesota			15		4	33	317	95	1,627	397	1,184

TABLE 12 (continued)

Institution	Ancient	Near Eastern	Far Eastern	Medieval	Renaissance and Baroque	18th–19th century	20th century	Drawings	Prints	Decorative arts	Other (Pre-Columbian, African, etc.)
Nebraska	5	3	44	5	10	25	317	118		73	
N.Y.U.							200	15	30		
North Carolina	145	80	2	25	5	10	10	40	5,000	200	4
Oberlin			2,220		113	138	123	195	850	1,775	20
Ohio State			1	1				4	170	15	11
Princeton	7,500	50	1,500	250	300	400	300	5,000	5,000	1,500	200
Smith	19	20	125	10	57	240	340	517	2,067	436	49
Vassar	3		968	11	55	152	118	256	637	4	28
Washington (St. Louis)	60	2	100		10	106	121	17	299	92	5
Williams	412	2	1	34	29	38	60	42	575	327	50
Wisconsin	1	12	9	2	74	97	67	35	519	50	39
Yale	2,000	2,000	2,000	50	200	800	300	2,000	13,000	5,000	1,500

TABLE 13 Percentage of gallery space devoted to various functions

Institution	Total square feet	Exhibition	Storage	Offices	Technical services	Classroom	Studio	Other (library, slide room, etc.)
Arizona	19,000	75	12.5		12.5			
U.C.L.A.	5,000	87	5	4	4			
Georgia	19,000	75	15	5	5			
Harvard	60,000	22.6	18.8	7.8	4.9	13	3	30
Illinois	17,000	43	23	5	16	13		
Indiana	24,000	50	30	10	10			
Iowa	4,000	92	8					
Kansas	22,000	49	20	5	6	15		
Michigan	20,000	60	25	10	5			
Nebraska	44,530	38	11	5	7	10.5		28.5
North Carolina	8,000	30	5	10	7	6		12
Oberlin	18,000	48	18	6.9	6.4		30	20.7
Princeton	60,000	75	15	10				
Smith	7,000	70	11	8	11			10
Vassar	9,000	61	26	3				
Washington (St. Louis)	11,000	78	22					
Williams	15,000	48	3	7	4	16	19	3
Yale	60,000	54	34	7	5			

TABLE 14   Art museum staff

Institution	Adminis-tration	Curatorial	Maintenance and security	Docentry
Arizona	1	2	2	
U.C.L.A.	3	2	2	
Georgia	2			
Harvard	15	15	10	
Illinois	4		3	
Indiana	1	1	2	
Iowa	1	1	1	
Kansas	2	1	1	
Michigan	5	3	2	
Nebraska	2		1	
North Carolina	1	1	3	
Oberlin	1	2	2	
Princeton	2	2	2	
Smith	3	2	1	
Vassar	1	1	3	
Washington (St. Louis)		1	1	
Williams	2		1	
Yale	10	13	10	2

Questionnaire

NOTE: Responses to questions should not take into consideration non-matriculated, correspondent, or extension students.

1. Name of college or institution _____

2. Enrollment (fall)

	1940-41	1950-51	1961-62
(1) undergraduate (male)			
(2) undergraduate (female)			
(3) graduate (male)			
(4) graduate (female)			

3. Total faculty

	1940-41	1950-51	1961-62

4. Total university expense budget

	1940-41	1950-51	1961-62

143

DEPARTMENT: General

1. Name of respondent

2. Position and title

General Information

3. Title of your department

4. Please give the 1961-62 expenses of your department on the table below. If possible restrict the use of the "combined program" column to those cases where expenses cannot be separated into "history of art" and "studio program"

	history of art	studio program	combined program

Administration

(1) salaries (administration only)

(3) office supplies and postage			
(4) telephone			
(5) equipment			
(6) equipment reserve			
(7) membership in professional organizations, subventions, etc.			
(8) publications (bulletin, catalogue)			
(9) scholarly publications			

Instruction

(10) salaries

(a) permanent faculty			
(b) term faculty			
(c) visiting faculty			
(d) assistants in instruction (teaching fellows)			

	history of art	studio program	combined program
(e) readers			
(f) occasional lecturers or critics			
(11) furniture and equipment (including audio-visual)			
(12) furniture and equipment reserve			
(13) supplies			
(14) travel			
(15) faculty research and publication assistance			
(16) student research and dissertation assistance			
(17) services purchased			
(18) miscellaneous			
Total			

5. What was the annual operating budget of your department, including salaries and wages, in

    (1) 1950-51 _____

    (2) 1940-41 _____

6. What was the total salary and wage budget of your department in

    (1) 1950-51 _____

    (2) 1940-41 _____

7. If your department serves only a part of your college or institution, what is the name of that part of your college or institution which is directly served by your department and roughly how large is its total enrollment

name _____

enrollment	1961-62	1950-51	1940-41
(1) male			
(2) female			

147

8. Faculty, 1961-62

	full-time faculty	part-time faculty	full-time equivalent of part-time faculty	current salary range at your college or institution
(1) professor				
(2) associate professor				
(3) assistant professor				
(4) instructor				
(5) lecturer				
(6) teaching assistant				
(7) guest lecturer or critic				
(8) other (specify)				

9. What percentage of your faculty teaching time is devoted to

(1) undergraduate instruction _____ %

(2) graduate instruction _____ %

10. **How many full-time faculty members did your department have in**

(1) 1950-51 _____

(2) 1940-41 _____

11. **What is the average teaching assignment for full-time members of your department expressed in classroom hours per week**

	art history	studio program
(1) 1961-62		
(2) 1950-51		
(3) 1940-41		

12. How many of your faculty members hold the degree of

    (1) PhD _____

    (2) MFA _____

    (3) MA _____

    (4) BFA _____

    (5) other (foreign) _____

13. How many of your faculty teach in other programs

    (1) general education _____

    (2) American studies _____

    (3) English _____

    (4) psychology _____

150

(5) sociology _____

(6) history _____

(7) economics _____

(8) other (specify) _____

14. **How much scholarship aid is currently given each year by your institution or department**

	total amount	number of scholarships	range of scholarships	size of average scholarship
studio program				
(1) undergraduate				
(2) graduate				
history of art				
(3) undergraduate				
(4) graduate				

151

15. How much loan assistance is currently given each year by your institution or department

	total amount available	total amount loaned	number of loans	range of loans	size of average loan
studio program					
(1) undergraduate					
(2) graduate					
history of art					
(3) undergraduate					
(4) graduate					

16. How many foreign students do you have as

(1) undergraduate majors _____

(2) graduate students _____

17. Are there other departments or divisions at your institution offering art courses (specify)

_____

_____

_____

18. If in addition to its regular academic program your department offers extension classes or correspondence programs, how many students are served by such courses (1961-62) _____

19. If your department offers regular summer sessions in art

    (1) how many students are enrolled in the summer sessions (1961-62) _____

    (2) how many of your faculty members teach in the summer sessions (1961-62) _____

    (3) how many outside faculty teach in the summer sessions (1961-62) _____

HISTORY OF ART

Questions relating to the art library, slides and photographs are placed at the end of this section. They are printed on separate sheets in order that you may have them answered by your librarian if you wish.

1. Name of respondent _____

2. Position and title _____

3. Name of college or institution _____

4. Does your department offer

(1) one introductory survey course _____

(2) several introductory survey courses _____

5. To which of the following general types do your introductory courses conform

	length: qtr/sem/yr	hours per week	offered annually
(1) historical survey			
(2) non-historical, topical survey			
(3) other			

6. How large is the average current enrollment in each of your introductory courses _____

7. What was the average enrollment in your introductory courses in

(1) 1950-51 _____

(2) 1940-41 _____

155

8. Are your introductory courses taught as

   (1) lectures _____

   (2) lectures and discussion _____

   (3) lectures and studio _____

9. How many faculty members participate in your introductory course program

   (1) professors _____

   (2) associate professors _____

   (3) assistant professors _____

   (4) instructors _____

   (5) assistants in instruction _____

   (6) other (specify) _____

10. What is the average enrollment in introductory courses at your college or institution in

(1) English _____

(2) history _____

(3) history of music _____

11. What subject at your college or institution has the largest introductory course enrollment _____
    What is the enrollment _____

12. Please list the titles of courses intended primarily for undergraduates offered regularly by your department in the following fields (omit courses listed in the catalogue which have not actually been given during the past three years and which are not likely to be given in the immediate future). Please indicate whether the courses are lecture courses or seminars and whether they are offered for one term only or for the full year

(1) Ancient art

lecture	seminar	term	year

157

	lecture	seminar	term	year
(2) Medieval art				
(3) Renaissance art				
(4) art of the seventeenth and eighteenth centuries				
(5) art of the nineteenth century				

158

(6) art of the twentieth century

(7) art of particular cultures or nations (i.e. Chinese art, Latin American art, Dutch seventeenth century art, etc.)

(8) history of particular branches of the arts (i.e. drawing, architecture, etc.)

(9) particular disciplines in art history or archaeology

	lecture	seminar	term	year

(10) other (specify)

_____

13. Number of students taking courses in your department (Fall, 1961) _____

14. Number of students graduating with a major in your department   (1) 1961-62 _____   (2) 1950-51 _____   (3) 1940-41 _____

15. What are the requirements for a major in your department.

_____

16. Are majors in the history of art required to take any studio work _____

17. What proportion of your students are taking a course in your department as a free elective _____

18. What proportion of your students are taking a course in your department as part of a definite program in some other area _____

19. From what other areas do students most frequently elect to minor in your field _____

Graduate Program

20. If you do not award graduate degrees please indicate here whether or not you offer courses for graduate students of other departments, and omit the remainder of the questions in this section

21. Please list the titles of courses intended primarily for graduate students offered regularly by your department in the following fields (omit courses listed in the catalogue which have not actually been given during the past three years and which are not likely to be given in the immediate future). Please indicate whether the courses are lecture courses or seminars, and whether they are offered for one term only or for the full year

	lecture	seminar	term	year
(1) Ancient art				
(2) Medieval art				
(3) Renaissance art				

(4) art of the seventeenth and eighteenth centuries

(5) art of the nineteenth century

(6) art of the twentieth century

(7) art of particular cultures or nations (i.e. Chinese art, Latin American art, Dutch seventeenth century art, etc.)

163

	lecture	seminar	term	year

(8) history of particular branches of the arts (i.e. drawing, architecture, etc.)

(9) particular disciplines in art history, archaeology or museology

(10) other (specify)

164

22. Which of the following degrees does your department offer   (1) PhD _____   (2) MA _____   (3) other (specify) _____

23. What are your basic departmental requirements for

(1) PhD	(2) MA	(3) other degrees offered

24. What is the total enrollment (1961-62) in the graduate program offered by your department _____

25. Number of advanced degree candidates in your department

	1961-62	1950-51	1940-41
(1) PhD			
(2) MA			
(3) other (specify)			

26. Please append a list of doctorates awarded since 1930, and the titles of the recipients' PhD dissertations

27. How many MA degrees has your department awarded since 1930 _____

28. How many years does it actually take the average candidate to obtain each of the following degrees

(1) PhD _____   (2) MA _____   (3) other (specify) _____

29. Does your department offer courses involving

(1) foreign travel _____   (2) archaeological field work _____   (3) study trips to museums _____

30.. In the past year how many graduate students in art history cut short their studies to

(1) switch to other fields _____ (2) accept art historical work for which higher degrees are not required _____ (3) marry _____

(4) other (specify) _____

31. Give a rough estimate of career choices by graduate students of your department who received only an MA within the past five years

(1) university teaching _____% (2) other teaching _____%

(3) museum (a) curatorial and administration work_____% (b) education_____%

(4) other (specify)_____%

32. Give a rough estimate of career choices by graduate students of your department who have received a PhD within the past five years

(1) university teaching_____% (2) other teaching _____%

(3) museum (a) curatorial and administration work _____% (b) education_____%

(4) other (specify) _____

Art Library

33. What is the total number of art books in your college or institution libraries _____

34. How many of these are housed in your departmental library rather than in other libraries _____

35. What is the annual circulation of art books

    (1) in your institution _____

    (2) in your departmental library _____

36. What is the annual budget for the purchase of art books

    (1) in your institution _____

(2) in your departmental library _____

37. **What percent of your annual budget for the purchase of art books comes from**

(1) your college or institution _____ %

(2) other sources (specify)_____ %

38. **Does your library subscribe to** <u>Art Index</u> _____

39. **Does your library contain copies of**

(1) Thieme-Becker, <u>Allgemeines Lexikon der Bildenden Kunstler</u> _____

(2) Thieme-Becker, <u>Kunstler Lexikon des Zwanzigsten Jahrhunderts</u> _____

40. Please indicate the periodicals to which your library currently subscribes

Check

(1) ____ Academie des Inscriptions et Belles-Lettres. Paris. Monuments et Memoires

(2) ____ American Academy in Rome. Memoirs

(3) ____ American Artist

(4) ____ American Fabrics

(5) ____ American Institute of Architects. Journal

(6) ____ American Institute of Planners. Journal

(7) ____ Antiquity

(8) ____ Aperture

(9) ____ Apollo

(10) ____ Archaeologia

(11) ____ Archaeology

(12) ____ Architectural Forum

(13) ____ Architectural Record

(14) ____ Architectural Review

(15) ____ L'Architecture d'Aujourd'hui

Check

(40) ____ Canadian Art

(41) ____ Casabella

(42) ____ Chicago. Art Institute. Quarterly

(43) ____ Cincinnati Art Museum. Bulletin

(44) ____ Cleveland Museum of Art. Bulletin

(45) ____ College Art Journal

(46) ____ Congres Archeologique

(47) ____ Connoisseur

(48) ____ Cooper Union. Museum. Chronicle

(49) ____ Craft Horizons

(50) ____ Design (British)

(51) ____ Design for Industry (formerly: Art & Industry)

(52) ____ Design Quarterly

(53) ____ Detroit Institute of Arts. Bulletin

(54) ____ Deutsches Archaeologisches Institut. Mitteilungen

(55) ____ Domus

(56) ____ Expedition

Check

(81) ____ Museums Journal

(82) ____ Oberlin College. Allen Memorial Art Museum. Bulletin

(83) ____ L'Oeil

(84) ____ Old-Time New England

(85) ____ Oriental Art

(86) ____ Oud-Holland

(87) ____ Pantheon

(88) ____ Perspecta

(89) ____ Philadelphia Museum of Arts. Museum Bulletin

(90) ____ Princeton University Art Museum. Record

(91) ____ Print

(92) ____ Printing & Graphic Arts

(93) ____ Progressive Architecture

(94) ____ Quadrum

(95) ____ Renaissance News

(96) ____ Revue Archeologique

(97) ____ Revue des Arts

171

Slide Collection

41. Do you maintain a slide collection _____

42. Is it administered by your department or by the university library _____

43. How many slides are there in your collection

(1) 3¼" x 4" black and white _____

(2) 3¼" x 4" color _____

(3) 2" x 2" black and white _____

(4) 2" x 2" color _____

44. What is the annual circulation of slides _____

45. Will A lo you department's current average annual expenditure for the purchase of slides

46. How many slides do you add to your collection annually _____

47. How many of these slides that you acquire each year do you

	all	most	half	some	none
(1) make yourself					
(2) purchase from outside sources					

Photographs and Reproductions

48. Does your department maintain a collection of mounted photographs and reproductions _____

49. How many photographs and reproductions does your department own _____

50. What is the annual circulation of photographs and reproductions _____

51. What is your department's current average annual expenditure for the purchase of photographs and reproductions _____

STUDIO PROGRAM

CAA   Q-4

1. Name of respondent _____

2. Position and title _____

3. Name of college or institution _____

Undergraduate Program

4. What fields of concentration do you offer and what is the enrollment in each

	offered	enrollment
(1) painting		
(2) sculpture		
(3) industrial design		

(4) graphic design (commercial design, advertising design)

(5) graphic arts (printmaking)

(6) crafts

(7) art education

(8) other (specify)

5. Please list the titles of courses intended primarily for undergraduate students offered regularly by your department in the following fields (omit courses which have not been given during the past three years and which are not likely to be given in the immediate future). Please indicate whether the courses are introductory or advanced in nature and whether they are offered for one term only or for the full year

	introductory	advanced	term	year
(1) painting				

CAA   Q-4

	introductory	advanced	term	year
(2) sculpture				
(3) industrial design				
(4) graphic design (commercial design, advertising design)				

(5) graphic arts (printmaking)

(6) crafts

(7) art education

(8) other (specify)

177

6. Number of students taking courses in your department (Fall, 1961) _____

7. Number of students graduating with a major in your department   (1) 1961-62 _____   (2) 1950-51 _____   (3) 1940-41 _____

8. What are the requirements for a major in your department

_____

_____

_____

_____

_____

_____

_____

_____

_____

178

9. What is the maximum number of studio courses that a major is allowed to take _____

10. If majors in your department are required to take courses in art history, what is the minimum requirement _____

11. What proportion of your students are taking a course in your department as a free elective _____

12. What proportion of your students are taking a course in your department as part of a definite program in some other area _____

13. From what other areas do students most frequently elect to minor in your field _____

Graduate Program

14. If you do not award graduate degrees please indicate here whether or not you offer courses for graduate students from other departments, and omit the remainder of the questions in this section

_____

_____

_____

_____

179

15. What fields of concentration do you offer and what is the enrollment in each

	offered	enrollment
(1) painting		
(2) sculpture		
(3) industrial design		
(4) graphic design (commercial design, advertising design)		
(5) graphic arts (printmaking)		
(6) crafts		
(7) art education		
(8) other (specify)		

16. Please list the titles of courses intended primarily for graduate students offered regularly by your department in the following fields (omit courses which have not been given during the past three years and which are not likely to be given in the immediate future). Please indicate, whether the courses are introductory or advanced in nature and whether they are offered for one term only or for the full year

	introductory	advanced	term	year
(1) painting				

180

(2) sculpture

(3) industrial design

(4) graphic design (commercial design, advertising design)

181

	introductory	advanced	term	year
(5) graphic arts (printmaking)				
(6) crafts				
(7) art education				
(8) other (specify)				

17. What degrees does your department offer _____

18. What are the basic departmental requirements for these degrees

19. Number of advanced degree candidates in your department

	1961-62	1950-51	1940-41
(1) MFA			
(2) other (specify)			

20. How many degrees has your department awarded since 1930

(1) MFA _____

(2) other (specify) _____

21. How many years does it actually take the average candidate to obtain the following degrees

(1) MFA _____

(2) other (specify) _____

22. What is the total enrollment (1961-62) in the graduate program offered by your department _____

23. Give a rough estimate of career choices by students of your department who have graduated within the last five years

   (1) independent creative work only _____ %

   (2) university or college teaching _____ %

   (3) professional school teaching _____ %

   (4) elementary, secondary or private school teaching _____ %

   (5) museum work _____ %

   (6) commercial work _____ %

   (7) other (specify) _____

185

UNIVERSITY ART MUSEUM

CAA   Q-5

1. Name of respondent _____

2. Title _____

3. Name of college or institution _____

4. Please enter the 1961-62 income and expenses of your museum

Income

(1) university appropriation _____

(2) endowment _____

(3) gifts _____

(4) sales (publications, etc.) _____

(5) other (specify) _____

Total _____

Expenses

(1) salaries (including social security, retirement allowance, etc.)   _____

    (a) administration   _____

    (b) curatorial   _____

    (c) maintenance and guards   _____

(2) furniture and equipment   _____

(3) furniture and equipment reserve   _____

(4) office supplies, postage and freight (excluding special exhibitions)   _____

(5) curatorial and maintenance supplies   _____

(6) travel   _____

(7) telephone   _____

(8) entertainment   _____

(9) acquisitions (excluding special gifts and receipts)   _____

(10) insurance (excluding special exhibitions)   _____

(11) lectures   _____

(12) care of collections   _____

(13) special exhibitions (including insurance, transportation, publication)   _____

(14) publications (excluding special exhibitions)   _____

(15) photography   _____

(16) subscriptions and memberships   _____

(17) services purchased   _____

(18) building (maintenance, care, utilities, etc.)   _____

(19) miscellaneous

Total   _____

5. What per cent of your acquisition budget is provided by your college or university _____ %

6. What is the net income produced by your membership program _____

7. How is this income used

_____

8. What is the size of your museum staff

(1) administrative _____

(2) curatorial _____

(3) maintenance and protection _____

(4) docent _____

9. How many square feet does your museum contain _____

190

10. What per cent of this space is devoted to

(1) exhibition _____ %

(2) storage _____ %

(3) offices _____ %

(4) technical services (workshop, photography, conservation, etc.) _____ %

(5) classroom _____ %

(6) studio _____ %

(7) other (specify) _____ %

191

11. Please describe and evaluate your collection as follows

number of objects	relative quality			
	excellent	good	fair	poor

(1) Ancient art

(2) Near eastern art

(3) Oriental art

(4) Medieval art

	number of objects	relative quality			
		excellent	good	fair	poor
(5) Renaissance and Baroque painting and sculpture					
(6) painting and sculpture of the eighteenth and nineteenth centuries					
(7) painting and sculpture of the twentieth century					
(8) drawings					
(9) prints					
(10) decorative arts					
(11) other (Pre-Columbian, African, etc.)					

12. In 1961-62 what per cent of your accessions were acquired by

(1) gift _____

(2) purchase _____

13. Does the museum produce a periodical publication such as a museum bulletin containing scholarly articles _____

14. If so, approximately what per cent of the articles is produced by

(1) museum staff   _____ %

(2) faculty   _____ %

(3) students   _____ %

(4) general outside contributors   _____ %
(museum curators, collectors, dealers, etc.)

15. Rank the needs of your museum

(1) _____ new acquisitions

(2) _____ additional personnel

(3) _____ exhibition space

(4) _____ storage space

(5) _____ office space

(6) _____ lecture rooms or auditorium

(7) _____ publication funds

(8) _____ travel funds for staff members below the rank of director

(9) _____ temporary loan exhibitions

(10) _____ research on permanent collections

(11) _____ other (specify)

193

16. Do other departments (archaeology, anthropology, library, etc.) within the university maintain art collections of any kind. Please specify.

_____

_____

_____

_____

_____

17. Please discuss any specific plans for the museum now under way with respect to

(1) building _____

_____

_____

(2) staff _____

_____

(3) program _____

18. What would be your ideal program for the future development of your art museum.

195